New
Habits

D

KT-177-105

30131 05339519 7

LONDON BOROUGH OF BARNET

A unique and courageous story of a fabulous and feisty woman moving from the constraints of a convent to the hedonism of the sixties. A tale of feminism, motherhood and courage.

Emma Freud OBE, broadcaster and social commentator

From a secluded world of abstinence and spiritual searching, Eleanor walked out into challenge, disappointment, health problems, relationship ups and downs – in fact, a life familiar to most of us! Her practical, sometimes faltering response, along with a healthy dose of humility and humour, contributes to this heartwarming tale of love, resilience and hope for us all.

Pam Rhodes, writer and broadcaster

New Habits

ELEANOR STEWART

LION

For John, Esme and Paul

Text copyright © 2015 Eleanor Stewart
This edition copyright © 2015 Lion Hudson

The right of Eleanor Stewart to be identified as
the author of this work has been asserted by her in
accordance with the Copyright, Designs and Patents
Act 1988.

All rights reserved. No part of this publication
may be reproduced or transmitted in any form or
by any means, electronic or mechanical, including
photocopy, recording, or any information storage
and retrieval system, without permission in writing
from the publisher.

Published by Lion Books
an imprint of
Lion Hudson plc
Wilkinson House, Jordan Hill Road,
Oxford OX2 8DR, England
www.lionhudson.com/lion

ISBN 978 0 7459 5668 8
e-ISBN 978 0 7459 5669 5

First edition 2015

A catalogue record for this book is available from
the British Library

Printed and bound in the UK, January 2015, LH26

Contents

Acknowledgments

To Di and Dee, who helped me remember so much. Thanks for all the giggly lunches. To my editor, Ali Hull, for her tireless help and encouragement, and to all the members of the Lion Hudson team, who are such a pleasure to work with.

Prologue

In September 1961, aged eighteen, I went to France to enter the Noviciate of the Sisters of Charity of Our Lady of Evron with the intention of becoming a nun and dedicating my life to God. After two and a half years I took my vows and a short time later returned to their main English convent, Mary-Mount in Liverpool. As a nun and encouraged by the Mother Superior, I became a student nurse, leaving my convent every day for Broadgreen, a big inner-city hospital, and returning each evening to my religious community. After qualifying as a registered nurse I trained for my midwifery diploma at the Liverpool Maternity Hospital. These were wonderfully happy years. I was contented and fulfilled. I enjoyed the community life and felt empowered by my vows. At all times I was surrounded by affectionate support from my sisters.

However, during my midwifery training I began to feel an immense desire to have a family of my own: a husband and children. I remained faithful to my vows, but became convinced that my life was turning in a different direction. In 1969, after eight years in a convent, I left the community. The sisters continued to be loving and supportive; I faced no antipathy, only sympathy.

The story of my life during those years is told in my book *Kicking the Habit*. What follows is my new life after the convent and my efforts to find my place in the modern world.

PART 1

Adaptation: Chichester
1969–70

CHAPTER 1

Homecoming

The girl sitting opposite me blew out her cheeks, raised her eyebrows, examined her fingernails and, rustling in her bag, produced her cigarettes. Taking one out, she lit it, inhaled deeply, then turning her head, presumably to avoid my face, blew a steady puff of blue smoke toward the window. When she turned back toward me, she was grinning. "Tell me again. Eight years? You were in a convent for eight years? You've got a lot of catching up to do."

Once the train pulled out of Liverpool's Lime Street station, she had begun to interrogate me with great persistence. Mother Henrietta's robust recommendations about finding a husband before I embarked on motherhood, which my travel companion had obviously overheard, had left me in a state of shock, but it had galvanized her curiosity and I faced a barrage of questions. She sat forward, crossing and re-crossing her legs, her shiny silky knees rubbing against each other. The sound was intimate and secret, as if her limbs were making quiet little murmurs of astonishment. My neat grey suit and pretty green blouse, chosen for me by Sister Mary, which I had thought smart, suddenly felt dowdy. My skirt was far longer than my companion's, which appeared to me extraordinarily brief. Every time she moved, it rode up a little more, revealing an expanse of plump brown thigh.

In an effort to turn the conversation away from what I felt would become prurient or more than inquisitive, I said, "Your tights are a pretty colour."

"American Tan; it's the new thing." She looked doubtfully at mine. "Yours are a bit pale, if you don't mind me saying so." She obviously felt that this unasked-for sartorial opinion would be acceptable to me, given my status as an ex-nun. For the next half an hour I was subjected to a persistent inquisition about convent life in general, and my own role in particular.

It was irritating, but I suppose not unreasonable. It's not every day that one comes across an ex-nun and one whose ex-status is so new, so her curiosity was understandable.

"Would you like a drink?" She was on her feet before I could reply. "There's a buffet car on the train."

"Thank you. A cup of tea would be lovely. Can I give you some money?"

"No, no! Don't go away. I've got lots more to ask." Outside in the corridor, she pushed cheerfully past standing passengers waiting for their stop. "Excuse me. Excuse me..." her voice faded as she disappeared from view. If I strained my ears, I could still hear her chattering away in the distance and I could only imagine what she might be saying: "You'll never guess – I'm in a carriage with an ex-nun." She was obviously finding the whole thing an exotic experience.

She arrived back with tea in one hand and something else in the other.

"That's not tea," I said.

"No," she grinned at me. "It's G and T."

"G and T?" It was so long since I had heard the abbreviation that I had forgotten it.

"Gin and tonic. Gosh, you don't know much, do you? And there's not too much tonic in it either. So..." she crossed her legs again and her nyloned knees whispered like old ladies sniggering behind their hands, "... where were we?"

As the details of convent life are, in the main, extraordinarily mundane I think my interrogator was beginning to feel some disappointment. It is difficult to explain to someone who has absolutely no knowledge of the religious life just what it involves: a community life, in all its simplicity, its order, its discipline, and the vows.

"I've seen *The Nun's Story*. Is it like that?" I'd often been asked this, and I guessed that she would pose the question too.

"No, nothing like it really."

"What about whipping yourself? Do you have to do that?"

"No, not in my community."

"What do you mean, 'not in my community'? Do some nuns do it?"

"Yes, some do, but it's not a big issue. It's mainly symbolic." Almost nobody asked about obedience or poverty, but all were fascinated about the absence of men, and by men they meant sex. It seemed to most people that the lack of sex was a major stumbling block and one that they imagined (erroneously) would be the hardest aspect of a nun's life.

By the time my tormentor left the train at Birmingham, I felt exhausted and was only too thankful to sink back in my seat and hope to be left in peace. Nobody came to disturb me, but the curious glances from passengers passing my carriage convinced me that my erstwhile companion had indeed spread the word. I decided there and then that I would keep very quiet about my past and recent life, unimpeachable as it was.

It was about 6:30 p.m. when I got to Euston, and by the time I had crossed London to catch the Portsmouth connection at Waterloo, I found I had missed it. I was concerned that my mother, in those pre-mobile phone days – and who didn't have a landline in her flat anyway – would be worried. As there was nothing I could do, I bought a sandwich and then went into a bar and daringly ordered a G and T. There were only a couple of other people inside, so the barman served me quickly. I looked dubiously at the small amount of gin in the glass and asked, "Is that all I get? Can I have a little more?"

"You want a large one? You should have said."

He returned my glass to the optic and gave it another shot. I took my drink and poured in some tonic. I nearly choked as the spirit struck the back of my throat. I managed not to cough, but when I looked up, the barman was grinning at me. "I guess it's not your tipple."

I turned my head away with embarrassment, but when I looked

back he was still smiling and said in a friendly sort of way, "Why don't you have something else?" He took the glass and bottle of tonic from me. "Go on, what do want?"

Memories of the feast-day Babycham at Mary-Mount made me smile, but I decided against asking for one of those. "I'll have a Scotch; a Scotch and soda." It seemed to define my new life and was a neat reference to my pre-nun days when I occasionally had such a drink with my father. It tasted blissful.

The train journey to Portsmouth was uneventful – no further interrogations! As the train drew into the station, my carriage slid past my mother sitting on a platform bench. She was a very small figure huddled in a pale, fluffy sort of coat. Her head was lowered and she looked vulnerable. I hoped she hadn't been waiting long. It was about 9 p.m. and chilly. She looked up as the train slowed to a stop. I walked toward her smiling, but she looked straight past me, her face anxious, and I realized with shock that she didn't recognize me. It was eight years since she had seen me in anything other than the habit.

"Mummy, it's me!"

She gave a gasping cry, in which joy and astonishment were mingled. Then she was hugging me and laughing, her hands tugging at my shoulders and caressing my cheeks. All the way to the taxi rank she held my hand in her soft little one and gazed, smiling, up at me.

Her bedsit was neat and charming but very small: a single bed, two small fireside chairs, a little table, a chest of drawers, a built-in wardrobe and, in an alcove, a tiny kitchenette, with a very neat electric cooker and a washbasin that served as a sink. She shared a bathroom at the end of the passage, she told me. I wondered where I would sleep. Looking around I admired the pretty curtains and matching bedspread that she told me, with justifiable pride, she had made herself. I felt a sudden rush of anger against my father, who had made no effort at all to provide for her or support her. I remembered the large married quarters that she had always made so comfortable and elegant, and the pretty cottage they had bought in Oxfordshire. She had been an officer's wife who had always backed her husband loyally, forgiven his infidelity, tolerated, but not without anguish, his rashness with money, and when she most needed support and help, he had abandoned her with shameful callousness.

She saw the look on my face and said in a rush, "I'm quite comfortable here. You know, I don't want for anything. It's fine really."

I could only hug her and say quite truthfully, "You're wonderful."

"I've arranged temporary accommodation for you with Mrs Martin downstairs. She's got the basement flat and her daughter's away at the moment. Is that all right? It's just until we decide what to do – where we are going to live." The excitement had gone from her voice and she sounded anxious and flustered.

"Of course; it's perfect." I was uncertain where we were going from there. In the short time between my writing to her and actually coming south nothing had been decided about the future, but I felt a momentary trepidation about the plans that she seemed to be forming regarding a shared life together.

"I want to make a home for you; a proper home."

Listening to her, and watching her animated happy face as she bustled about setting the table in the window and putting together the things she needed for a meal, I didn't think it was the moment to tell her that this was the last thing I wanted. I was avid for independence. I didn't want to be mothered.

During the evening, after a late simple supper of baked potatoes and cold meat, she confessed that she had been made redundant, as the garage, where she had been in charge of the radio department, had closed. She needed, she said, to find other employment. I did a quick mental calculation and reckoned she must be about fifty-five years of age, young enough to be re-employed. She seemed quite optimistic about finding another job and as her mind was full of plans for what we ought to do, I let her chat on and just listened, smiling, my heart like lead in my chest. I couldn't think when the best moment would be to tell her that this was not at all what I had in mind.

Later, lying sleepless in the pleasant digs she had found for me, I began to have concerns about how I was to untangle this mare's nest. Then, exhausted by the emotion of the day, I plunged into sleep.

Life seemed a great deal more cheerful the following morning. We walked down to the seafront and looked across the water, watching the yachts dipping and turning through the bouncing waves. Ryde, on the Isle of Wight, looked like a toy town, the spire of the church glinting in the sun.

We found a small grubby café. The tables had the greasy feel, as if they had been wiped with an oily rag, but it was warm and the waitress friendly enough.

"You need some clothes," said my mother, and we spent an hour over coffee deciding what I should buy and making a list of essentials. She would have kitted me out from head to toe if I had let her, but eventually I persuaded her that underwear and a basic wardrobe would be adequate until I had gainful employment. My nun's dowry of £30 (in today's money about £400) had been returned to me when I left the community. It seemed a large sum, but this was what I had to live on till I found a job, and it had to cover rent, food and clothes. I knew I had to be cautious.

The inside of C&A in Commercial Road overwhelmed me. It was a dazzling emporium of light, colour and sound. So much variety, and when did they start to play music in shops? Lewis's department store in Liverpool, where I had bought my neat "leaving the convent" suit, was a gloomy cave by comparison. Here there was row upon row of garments in every shape, size and colour: dresses, tunics, skirts – short and long, straight and flared – trousers, shorts and blouses proliferated, shelves piled high with tee-shirts, jumpers, sweaters, cardigans, crocheted boleros and little leather jerkins. Many of the lighter summer things were made from what looked like muslin.

"Cheesecloth," I was informed. "All the girls are wearing it."

"But it's practically transparent!"

"Yes, isn't it pretty!"

I began to look at my mother with quite a new eye. How, I thought, would I ever know what to choose? I certainly couldn't imagine myself wearing cheesecloth.

After half an hour I was ankle deep in garments selected apparently at random by my determined parent. She held each one up against me and squinted at the effect. Some she discarded and tossed aside on the grounds of being "the wrong colour" or "not right for you", or sometimes, when I daringly suggested something, she would laugh and say, "No, Eleanor, that's dreadful." I realized she was in her element and I was reluctant to spoil her fun.

Eventually we had a pile of chosen garments, but when I realized she meant me to buy them all, I resisted. "I thought we were just going to select out of this lot." I was aghast. "Look, I don't need everything at once. A couple of skirts and blouses or tops, a dress, a jacket or light coat, Mummy. That's enough."

She gave in reluctantly but then swept me off to the lingerie department. "Underwear," she stated firmly. There we had the same scenario. By this time, the shop assistants were ecstatic, only too ready to make as many suggestions as possible, believing that they were seeing prodigal expenditure here. If they were on commission, they were going to do well. I was soon afloat in frothy pants, bras and negligees, and the changing rooms were rapidly taking on the appearance of how I imagined a high-class bordello would look. My mother told me later that it was one of the happiest mornings of her life.

"My money is limited until I get a job. I can only afford the minimum and I don't need *seven* bras," I told her.

"Of course you do, darling. There are seven days in a week. You need a clean one every day."

"Are you sure? It seems awfully excessive." I didn't want to confess in front of strangers that as a nun I had changed my bra once a week. This, I knew, would have seemed unacceptably unhygienic.

"Oh no, madam," interjected the assistant. "Seven is the bare minimum."

After some argument I paid for the clothes already selected and told my mother that Marks and Spencer was the place to go for underwear. In England, even as a nun we got our underwear from M&S! There I bought three double packs of perfectly serviceable cotton bras and matching pants.

"I'm sure you bought stuff like this when you were a nun," my mother said reproachfully, eyeing the simple nighties I also put into the basket.

Later that evening I tried my purchases on once again and felt satisfied with the results.

Not my mother. "All those skirts need taking up, and your grey suit is only wearable with a hem at least three inches shorter."

Before going to bed, she produced a C&A bag, announcing that I must have something pretty. "Serviceable; such an unattractive word," she said. Inside the bag were two enchanting lacy bras and matching briefs. "A welcome home present," she announced, kissing me.

I sat on my bed fingering the lovely frilly underwear and feeling very worldly and sophisticated. I needed shoes, I thought, and a coat, but that would be for another day.

Next morning, hanging outside my bedroom door, were two skirts, a pair of trousers and the grey suit, all beautifully taken up and pressed. She'd pinned a note on them: "Ready to wear". I realized she must have been up for hours, and was deeply touched and grateful. I wondered again how and when I could tell her about my own plans for the future.

Chapter 2

Problems

A few days after my arrival in Portsmouth, my mother announced that now was a good opportunity to move out of the town and find a flat somewhere else. "I've never liked Portsmouth," she announced, a statement that astonished me. One of the important things in her life was second-hand bookshops, of which there was an abundance in the city. "In a good bookshop," she once told me, "nobody should bother you; they should just leave you alone to browse." She was never happier than when she found a dusty corner where she could rummage and discover some ancient tome for which she would pay a tidy sum, particularly if it had what she described as "a nice little binding". Even in her tiny studio flat there were lots of books. All my life I have associated second-hand bookshops, with their particular fusty odour of dust, damp and old leather, with my mother. She had a good eye, so all through my young life on our shelves we had books whose provenance was as far from WHSmiths as it could be. I don't remember her ever buying a new book.

However, I had some sympathy when I thought about her desire to move. Portsmouth was where her marriage had imploded. She had become seriously unwell and her time as an inpatient in the local psychiatric hospital had not been voluntary. She was clearly envisaging a new life with a daughter rather than a husband.

A pleasant day spent in Chichester convinced her that this was the optimal place for us. I too found the city enchanting, and felt more than ready to move there, but the problem of explaining to her my need for a separate life was becoming acute. I knew the longer I left it, the harder it would be. My money was beginning to run thin: three weeks had passed since leaving Liverpool.

So we moved to Chichester. Still too reluctant to face up to her, we found what I sincerely hoped would be temporary accommodation: a boarding house on the outskirts of the city. In effect we were sharing a bedsit, a large and pleasant room but a bedsitter never the less. I looked around in dismay, while my mother appeared relentlessly cheerful. I was pretty sure I was going to find this situation intolerable. The room would have been fine for one; it was large, clean and airy. But two adults in the relatively confined space meant we were, neither of us, ever going to be on our own.

"We've got to find something better," I announced.

"Oh yes, once we settle in in Chichester, but this is fine for the moment."

I didn't think it was fine at all, not even for a moment, but there was little I could do. I felt dreadfully depressed. My courage had failed me in addressing the situation and this was so far from what I had envisaged when I left my convent. As I unpacked my still meagre belongings, listening to my mother humming happily, I was filled with an impotent fury at my helplessness. Why, I thought, had I been landed with this?

Things were worse at night. I had forgotten about my mother's restlessness and nocturnal smoking which, after a few nights, became almost unbearable. Then my old enemy, insomnia, returned, so both of us were tossing and turning. Sometimes I got up and made a cup of tea and we sat there, the two of us, in the dark, while she smoked in silence. Eventually desperate for sleep, we went back to bed. Poor creature, she had little control over her emotions. In fact, as I soon realized, the move and my arrival in her life had destabilized her, and she would burst into tears at the least thing – the difficulty of finding a launderette or running out of cigarettes – and would weep helplessly. I thought she was perfectly justified in her despair about this, but couldn't for the life of me think what to do about it. I seemed to spend my time comforting and reassuring her, once I'd found a launderette and bought her some cigarettes. Separation from her seemed less and less possible.

Some days were pleasant enough. We went once or twice to the Festival theatre and on one occasion saw an excellent production of *Anthony and Cleopatra*, my mother's favourite play. That kept her happy for a few days, but trying to remain upbeat was difficult. She was relying more and more on me for companionship and entertainment. One evening, desperate to fill the void of hours together, I suggested the cinema and chose at random a film called *Rosemary's Baby*. It was not at all like *The Sound of Music*, which all the nuns at Mary-Mount had been to see. I had never seen such explicit simulated sex on the screen before and was shocked. I half expected the cinema to be raided by the vice squad. The theme of the film was satanism, and I fully expected my mother, a good practising Catholic, to get up and leave. I was quite ready to go myself, but she sat placidly, eyes glued to the screen, apparently unfazed by all the writhing and groaning going on in front of us.

"Mummy," I hissed in her ear. "This film is about fornication and devil worship."

"Yes, I know, darling," she hissed back. "It's very good, isn't it?"

I was silent with astonishment. We discussed it, giggling, all the way back to our wretched digs. But these were rare moments.

Although I was busy organizing a working life, my mother was showing no inclination to find employment, so I assumed she was living on her meagre savings. Our rent was cheap, but our funds were depleting and I knew I needed to find work. I also needed to be away from her. The atmosphere in our bedsit was claustrophobic.

The *Midwives* journal gave two addresses for nursing agencies and one of them proposed the local hospital, St Richard's. The agency was helpful in every way. The salary, through an agency, was better than the NHS nursing scale and as money was significant I opted for that.

"My, they will be pleased to have you," the agency manageress assured me. "They are desperately short-staffed. The post is for a staff midwife. We don't provide a uniform, but a navy blue dress will do and a buckram belt. The hospital provides caps. Nothing frilly, I'm afraid, those dreadful paper ones, but you're entitled to your silver buckle. You might pick up one in a second-hand shop in The Hornet. It's a pleasant street full of quirky shops."

The silver buckle was the accepted badge of the qualified nurse. I was determined to find one, and picked up a pretty Indian silver clasp that my mother sewed onto my buckram belt. It had to be taken in regularly over the next three months as my weight dropped steadily to that of my pre-convent days, due to a combination of a less stodgy diet and stress. My mother, always cheerful when she was doing something with me, came shopping for the requisite navy dresses. By this time I had become a little more about shopping for clothes and personal things

I was much less confident about money matters. The nursing agency offered me an advance on my salary and asked for my bank details. As I didn't have a bank account, I was disconcerted and mumbled about not having any details on me. I didn't have the faintest idea about how to open an account. Eventually I plucked up courage and went into Lloyds. The teller was very helpful and advised me to go back to the agency and ask for a cheque.

"You see," she explained kindly, "you actually have to have some money in order to open an account. When you have the cheque, then come back to us and we can open an account for you."

An hour later, having secured the cheque, my account was opened. I was told that my cheque book would come in about a week. With cash in the bank and the prospect of a regular income, I felt flush with money. With the navy blue dresses, the buckram belt and my pretty buckle, I felt at last my new life was beginning.

In fact it was a fortnight before I started at St Richard's, as although I had my diploma certificates, nursing and midwifery, the agency was waiting for references. Time hung very heavily on my hands, and I was still struggling with the question of how to leave my mother.

I went to the maternity unit to meet the senior midwife in charge, Sister Baines. She looked to be on the verge of retirement but was friendly and welcoming.

"Yes, we could certainly do with more staff; when can you start?"

"As soon as my references arrive and I sign the contract. Probably next week."

"I really must find something to do," said my mother as I prepared for my first morning at the hospital. "Otherwise I can't think how I'll fill the day when you are at work." She was still showing no sign of looking for employment. I had stopped asking her, as she seemed very reluctant to address the issue. So I wasn't quite sure what she had in mind.

"What time do you expect to be home?" she queried as I dressed. She was still in bed. It was this sort of "needy" remark that made me feel trapped and resentful.

"I don't know," I snapped and, seeing the look of hurt on her face, was filled with helplessness. "I haven't got my hours yet. I'll know tomorrow."

CHAPTER 3

Employment

It was an easy fifteen-minute walk to the maternity unit, past the market and through the leafy, bucolic Priory Park, which ran below the city's Roman walls. I felt a rush of elation at both the freedom and the novelty of it all. Here at least I was running my own life, even if ineptly. I had failed to address the problem of my mother, I'd been apprehensive about a bank account and I didn't like my accommodation.

The spring weather was beautiful and the park full of flowers. People sometimes sneer at the choices of the local Parks and Gardens Department (as it was called then), with their planting of a surfeit of marigolds and pansies, but Chichester's public spaces were filled that spring with great drifts of daffodils and narcissi and, under the trees, there were carpets of blue and white crocuses. Those delightful spring flowers lifted my spirits and helped me to suppress any guilt I felt at leaving my mother on her own. I was certainly enchanted to be on *my* own. I had never felt so independent. I smiled happily at anyone I passed and even risked a chatty "Hello, lovely morning".

I had telephoned and written to Mother Henrietta, my last Mother Superior, and told her to send my signed request for dispensation from my vows to the Archbishop. I knew she had hung on to them for some weeks in the hope that I might come back to the community. Until they were ratified and sent to Rome, I was still part of the congregation. All she had to do was tear them up and I could return "home", but as soon as I left I knew that my decision was not only definitive but the right one. So that morning

I was light-hearted and optimistic.

St Richard's had started life in 1938 as a small hospital for the care of elderly sick people, but at the beginning of the war, it was expanded to cope with civilian casualties, and several Nissen-hutted wards were added. The maternity unit was of this type. Two Nissens were linked by a brick corridor. Externally its grim and utilitarian appearance was unfortunate, but inside it was bright, airy and pleasant. It was run with great efficiency by Sister Baines and her deputy, Sister Walters, both extremely experienced, and I joined a small group of midwives, nursery nurses and nursing auxiliaries. They seemed delighted to have me. "We've been so short staffed," they kept repeating. I felt immediately at home.

The unit had an antenatal and postnatal wards, several single rooms and two delivery rooms. There was the usual sluice room, echoing noisily with the ubiquitous bedpans and trollies, a clean preparation room, a large bright nursery, a very small, hot room with three incubators called somewhat pretentiously the "special care unit" (or SCU) for premature babies, a very small operating theatre for emergencies, and the sisters' office.

After Broadgreen Hospital where I had trained, and even the relatively intimate Liverpool Maternity Hospital where I had done my midwifery, this unit felt very small, but it was delightfully welcoming and had great charm. The curtains round the beds and the counterpanes were cheerfully coloured, there were flowers and congratulatory cards everywhere, and few rigid rules about patients coming and going, with greater relaxation in the afternoon about visiting times. Mornings, as usual in any hospital, were busier and filled with the business of doctors' rounds and tests or investigations.

In the sixties and seventies, most mothers having a baby for the first time remained in hospital after delivery for up to seven days. It was extremely uncommon for a mother to leave earlier. As a result, it was easier to form friendships – and lasting ones at that – and the postnatal wards tended to be rather jolly. Patients in early labour were looked after in the antenatal ward and then moved to a side ward when they needed pain relief, before being transferred to the delivery room. Those whose medical condition – diabetes or high blood pressure, for example – necessitated special treatment were automatically nursed in a single room.

Sister Walters, a quiet, pleasant woman, showed me around and explained the routine. It was all very familiar. I was only pulled up short when, in the delivery room, I suddenly realized that unless there was some complicating factor, I would be in charge. It would be my case and my responsibility. There would be no midwife to stand behind me, to supervise me, guide me or take over. My stomach lurched. Sister Walters saw my face.

"What's the matter?" she said. "Why are you looking so worried?"

"I was just thinking… you know, when I deliver someone, it's up to me. I've never delivered one on my own before."

She smiled reassuringly "Usually there are two of us anyway, but don't worry, we know you are new; you can always press the buzzer for help. It's much easier than you think. Most women left to their own devices give birth perfectly naturally; we are there just to catch the baby so to speak, and to make sure they don't fall off the couch. Delivery beds are quite narrow, aren't they?"

I had just seen a particularly large woman waddle past the door, so overweight that it was difficult to assess whether she was still pregnant or had actually given birth. I blenched at the thought of trying to catch just such a one.

"Yes, exactly," said Sister Walters, following my gaze.

As I got to know the other midwives, I realized that sometimes things were different from what I had been used to in Liverpool, so here too there was a "house style". The way the mothers were treated, the sort of pain relief offered, the length of time they were allowed to labour before any sort of intervention was considered necessary, even the milk used for the babies being bottle fed: none of these things were the same. They weren't worse or better, just different.

Staff midwives did not attend the antenatal clinics, which were held in the main outpatients department: Sister Baines and Sister Walters took them. This meant that the first time we met most patients was when they were admitted in labour. Any patients booked for a planned caesarean delivery were admitted to an antenatal ward the day before and then, on the day itself, were trundled across the bumpy car park to the theatre in the main block. This was no problem if the weather was fine but on rainy days the expectant mother, wrapped in a blanket and covered in a rubber sheet, would be escorted by someone from the unit, usually one of the auxiliaries, who struggled to hold an umbrella over her in a vain attempt to keep her dry. As the said escort would also be clasping the patient's notes and often had to contend with gusty wind, we all used to watch anxiously from the windows until the stretcher party disappeared out of sight. Sometimes the jolting and bumping was quite vigorous enough, I thought, to send the mother into labour before she reached the operating table.

All midwives new to the unit had to adjust to new routines, coming as we did from a variety of training hospitals.

"We deliver our mothers on their backs," Sister Baines explained. "It's the way our consultants like it."

I had been trained to deliver women lying on their left side. There were sound obstetric reasons for doing so. If a woman lay on her back, her heavy uterus could press down on the big vein, the inferior vena cava, that lay behind it, which could cause her blood pressure to fall. I didn't question this directive but I didn't think consultants' preference for a particular procedure was sufficient reason to follow it.

Most of the other midwives had been trained for longer than I had, were more experienced and some had been previously employed in far more exotic situations than I had ever known. Enid Baker, who came to lunch in the canteen with me on my first day at St Richard's, had been part of the medical team on the old *Queen Elizabeth* cruise ship and had worked subsequently on the *QE2*. "The old one had more style, was much classier," she told me. It sounded wonderfully romantic, being a nurse on an ocean-going liner.

Another girl had for six months been a private midwife to a member of the Scottish aristocracy. She had delivered the baby and then stayed on to take care of it. The house, she told us, smelled permanently of wet tweed and much wetter dog. "Even the baby's nappy, whatever the contents, had a peculiar odour of grouse or heather."

She was a pretty, sassy Irish girl, with long honey coloured hair and hazel eyes, and was called Amber, an appropriate name given her colouring. She had trained at the Mater Hospital in Belfast. There was something vaguely mysterious about her. She told us that she had a fiancé at home, but her subsequent outrageously flirtatious relationship with a very handsome Spanish employee of a local pub in North Street made us feel that it was not likely her engagement was built on very durable foundations. She always insisted that her friendship with Pedro was platonic. But we saw her on several occasions locked in close embrace and even in public she found it hard to keep from touching and stroking whatever handy part of him she could reach. She had a ground-floor room in the nurses' home, as she was on the staff and not an agency midwife. "Very convenient for climbing in and out," another nurse spitefully pointed out.

Rather to my dismay the unit worked the three-shift system, so the unpleasant split shift was once again part of my timetable, and every six weeks we had a week's night duty. But the working atmosphere was lovely and I settled down very quickly.

I had told nobody about my past, just saying I had been studying in France, and that I had trained in Liverpool. I managed to field the inevitable questions about the Beatles and Liverpool nightlife without too much difficulty and without having to resort to deception. One morning, however, going across to the main hospital on some errand, my past unexpectedly caught up with me. I saw a young man walking toward me up the long corridor. I recognized him straight away as a medical student I had worked with in Liverpool Maternity Hospital. Like my mother at the station, he didn't recognize me. I only hesitated momentarily. This unexpected apparition from my past was too great a temptation. After he passed me, I turned and called his name.

"Stuart!"

He turned to look enquiringly at me.

"Don't you recognize me?"

"Sorry... no," he smiled, but came a step or two toward me.

"It's me, Sister Stewart. From LMH."

He looked thunderstruck and was completely stunned for a moment. He began to utter, "Great Scot! My God! My Lord! What on earth are you doing here?"

"I'm not a nun any more," I said sheepishly. "I left my convent." As soon as the words were out of my mouth I regretted them. I rushed into the next sentence. "I live in Chichester. I've got a job here. Is this your first houseman job?"

"No, not really. I'm just a locum. I'm off tomorrow. I've got a houseman job in Cardiff. What an extraordinary chance to bump into you today!"

We chatted for a few minutes.

"Please don't tell anyone about me and Liverpool. I'm keeping it under my hat for the moment." I was relieved that he was leaving, as I thought the chances of him not telling people were slim, although he assured me solemnly, "Your secret is safe with me. Good luck... I can't believe it." He still looked bemused as he walked away. This episode rattled me a bit but I was still intent on discretion about my past. So I didn't mention this unexpected encounter back in the maternity unit.

On my first day off, I hesitantly asked Amber if she would like to come shopping with me. She agreed, and looked as horrified as my mother at some of my choices. With her advising me, though, I bought some pretty outfits and some beautiful shoes. My love affair with footwear began then, an addiction that has persisted. My favourite purchase was a pair of white knee-high boots with platform shoes, for which I paid £5 19s 11d; a very big expenditure at that time.

Thanks to Amber, who although taller than me was very slim, I discovered that we could both fit into some children's clothes, particularly skirts and jeans. Like my mother I was only five foot two. This was a great saving, as there was no purchase tax on them. It also meant that I could wear the briefest of miniskirts and the tightest of jeans and didn't have to shorten the leg, which was always annoying as it diminished the amount of flare! I loved the clothes with their geometric patterns and the swinging A-line dresses, but I had very little idea of what constituted a bargain. Without Amber to advise me, I would have made some rash purchases.

"You're buying an amazing amount of stuff," she said after another outing, as we sat down for a drink in a café near the cathedral.

"I haven't got very many clothes," I replied diffidently.

"It doesn't look as if you had anything; this is a complete new wardrobe!"

"Oh, you know: new place, new style," I laughed uneasily. She was beginning to remind me of the girl on the train.

"Speaking of style, you really should get rid of that dreadful grey suit I saw you in the other day. Where the hell did you get that?"

"I don't really know. I've had it for ages; just got used to it, I suppose."

"It doesn't look as if it's that old. It looks pretty new. But ditch it anyway."

Amber was sharp and she clearly suspected something. But as the likelihood of guessing the truth was remote, I felt relatively secure.

CHAPTER 4

A Fine but Brief Romance

The SCU nursery was all St Richard's could boast of in terms of intensive care. Seriously ill infants, or ones needing surgery, were transferred to other nearby hospitals that had the facilities to deal with them. This meant that our incubators were used, in the main, for premature babies, defined as any baby less than five pounds in weight and/or born before thirty-six weeks' gestation.

Many babies fitting those criteria were perfectly healthy and only needed a little more care and attention by their mothers and the nursery staff. But some very tiny babies were born, and these needed to stay in the unit, sometimes for several weeks. A baby delivered at thirty weeks (or sometimes at twenty-eight), weighing barely three pounds and sometimes a great deal less, would be seriously immature. In particular the lungs were not fully developed. These tiny creatures had poor muscle tone, difficulty regulating their own body temperature and were often not strong enough to suckle, so quite a lot of them were fed by tube. Mothers who went home, leaving babies behind, came in sometimes twice a day, often to do nothing other than caress their tiny tots through the incubators' windows. It was a wonderful moment when they could at last hold their babies in their arms, and even better if they could feed them.

Sometimes they brought in expressed breast milk, which we kept in the fridge in the little ward kitchenette. We were careful about labelling the bottles. Failure to do so meant that one risked putting breast milk into the tea, which was not to everyone's taste.

I had seen "prems" in Liverpool, but they were looked after

in the high-dependency nursery and I had had little to do with them. In St Richard's the midwives and the nursery nurses were heavily involved. Handling such tiny scraps was nerve-racking at first. Lifting, feeding, moving a baby whose tiny head, barely the size of a satsuma, didn't even fill my palm, was very challenging. It took some time before I could convince myself that they wouldn't break apart or evaporate each time I touched one. I could lift such an infant, cup its head, and lay it along my forearm, and the feet wouldn't even reach my elbow.

Despite my apprehension, I soon got used to dealing with them, although I still felt as if I were handling a tiny kitten. The smaller they were, the redder and hairier, their little bodies covered with a silky down called lanugo. This soft fluffy hair is characteristic of premature babies and is associated with low body mass. Strangely it is also present in people suffering from anorexia, for the same reason. Some of the very low birth weight infants did not survive and there was no heroic effort made to save them. Death was then an accepted and inevitable result of extreme prematurity.

Under our careful nursing, despite not going to the lengths normal in today's high-tech environment, a considerable number of these babies did survive. Kept warm, occasionally with added oxygen, together with light-therapy for the jaundice to which "prems" are very prone, and which can be a very serious issue, they clung to life with grim determination. The light-therapy gave the incubators and the nursery itself a strange, blue incandescent glow. It was spooky, particularly at night, with just the interior of the incubator illuminated, and I often had the impression that they were hovering in mid-air, like an alien spaceship enclosing embryonic aliens.

One morning, busily dealing with the routine feeding, I heard the door behind me open. I was expecting one of the nursery nurses, so didn't look around.

"Good morning." It was a lovely deep voice, a dark brown kind of voice, and when I turned around I found myself looking at a dark brown skinned man wearing a white doctor's coat. He smiled, eyes crinkling at the corners. "Good morning," he repeated. "I'm Jack

Arnold. I'm the locum paediatrician for a week. I thought I ought to drop in, make myself known, and look at these little people."

He was a big, broad-shouldered man, above average height with a straight narrow nose and a strong jaw line. I thought him extremely handsome, and guessed him to be in his mid-thirties. I couldn't place his accent but thought he might be South African. I was taken aback by his informality. Doctors either didn't bother to introduce themselves, expecting you to know who they were, or said nothing so that you had to peer at their name badge in the hope that you could decipher it. Occasionally they might deign to announce themselves, but always with the prefix "doctor".

His appearance was so unexpected that I didn't move and just looked at him. After a moment, smiling again, he gestured, "Excuse me." He nodded at the sink and moved toward it to wash his hands.

"I'm so sorry, doctor. Shall I get Sister Walters for you?"

"No need; I'm quite happy with you." He dried his hands and turned toward the incubators. He examined the babies, handling them with great sensitivity and talking to each one soothingly. "Hello, young lady, I'm Dr Arnold. I just want to check you over, listen to that bold little heart." Then on to the next one: "How's the breathing? I know the stethoscope's cold. I'm sorry. You were asleep, didn't want to be disturbed."

The infant in question began to wail. I always found it astounding how, when roused, even these tiny creatures managed to produce such an astonishing volume of noise. He looked up from his examination. "Can you tell me about them?"

"Yes, of course." I had just launched into, "This is Baby Harrison, delivered at thirty-one weeks' gestation..." when Sister Walters arrived, out of breath.

"I'm so sorry. I didn't know you were here. I've only just been informed. Staff Stewart, you should have let me know." Then, addressing him, she said reproachfully, "Doctors usually come to the office first."

"I'm sorry. I didn't know where the office was, but I saw the notice on this door, 'Prem. Baby Unit', so I thought I'd start here." The lovely crinkle-eyed smile flashed again. "But not to worry,

Staff Nurse has looked after me well. Perhaps I could see the notes?"

I was despatched to fetch them. When I got back, he was talking to Sister Walters in the passage but he followed me back into the room with her after him. He propped the papers up onto an incubator and began to write. When he had finished, he turned to her, nodded and said softly, "Thank you, Sister Walters."

She didn't move, just looked a little puzzled, so he passed the notes to her and, smiling gently, repeated, "*Thank you,* Sister Walters." The blood rushed up into her cheeks but she took the hint with good grace, glanced at me and left the room. Embarrassed, I looked down at the floor and then raised my head to face him. I felt at a complete loss. I saw a slight movement of his lips and thought he was amused at my discomfort.

"Is everything all right here, Dr Arnold?" I hoped I hadn't sounded too brusque, and cleared my throat.

"Perfectly all right. Are there any paediatric problems?"

"You should ask Sister Walters. I'm not in charge."

"Right, I'll come back tomorrow. Are *you* on duty tomorrow?"

His directness took me by surprise and I stammered, "Er, yes, yes I am."

"Then I'll see you in the morning. What's your name?"

"Staff Midwife Stewart."

He smiled again with a raised eyebrow and repeated, "What's your name?"

"Eleanor." I paused. He looked so confident, so self-assured, that I laughed. "Eleanor Stewart."

"Good. Then I'll see you tomorrow, Staff Midwife Eleanor Stewart." Then he was gone.

Mac, one of the nursing auxiliaries, stuck her head round the door. She was breathless with admiration. "Isn't he super!" she said. "He looked at all the other babies and asked *me* if there was any problem, *and* listened when I told him about Baby Wallace's sticky eye. A real charmer, I reckon."

Back in the office Sister Walters was telling Sister Baines, "I have never been so comprehensively dismissed. Isn't that right,

Staff Stewart? *Thank you, Sister Walters.* Talk about realizing when you're not wanted."

"What did he want to say to you that he didn't want Walters to hear?" another midwife, a pleasant, plump girl, queried over lunch. Enid and I looked at each other and smiled. Enid raised her eyebrows. "Dorothy! For goodness' sake," she said. "I expect he wanted a date. Use your imagination."

Dorothy was a sweet-natured girl, but naïve to an unbelievable degree and not strong on imagination. She developed a crush on each of our successive housemen and registrars in turn, and took to crocheting ties or, even worse, long multi-coloured scarves that she called "mufflers" for them. They were presented with excruciating coyness, and received with embarrassment and dismay. She was an excellent midwife, hardworking and committed, and popular with the patients, but she seemed to belong to another decade, the fifties or even the early forties. Everything about her was old-fashioned, both her appearance and her manner, and she was often the butt of our wit – teasing that she took in good part. She lived with her mother, and I envied her the tranquil life they seemed to have together, but was infuriated by her surprise that I found my own situation so problematic.

"All it needs is a bit of give and take," she declared easily, crocheting away. This statement had me grinding my teeth.

"Look," I said. "You and your mother live in a three-bedroomed house. You drive a car and your mother belongs to the WI and the Townswomen's Guild. She has lots of her own interests. I live in a bedsit with mine and she has no interest in anything at the moment, apart from what I do. It's not the same! And currently I'm doing all the giving and my mother is doing all the taking!"

Walking back to the bedsit that I had taken to calling secretly "the cage", I passed the modern, ugly Catholic church and went in. I was immediately enveloped in the comforting odour of polish and incense, and sat down. The Curate of Ars, St John Vianney, was once asked what he said to God on his numerous visits to church. "I don't say anything," he replied. "I look at him and he looks at me." That evening I did the same and came out calmer, but I said nothing to my mother, whom I found chatting affably to our landlord, either about my visit to the church or about the incident in the special baby care unit. She seemed happier and I didn't want to put a spoke in the wheel.

The following morning I was kept busy monitoring a girl in labour and by about ten o'clock I was in the delivery room with her. I had no time to think about Dr Jack Arnold. Her baby was born shortly after midday, and when I had finished cleaning up and my patient was back in bed with her infant snuggled down in its crib beside her, I went into the office to write up the notes.

Dr Arnold was sitting casually on the edge of the desk, chatting to Sister Baines. He got up when I arrived and gave me his crinkly eyed smile. He didn't speak, just looked at me, but Sister Baines, obviously not wishing to be as summarily dismissed as Walters had been the previous day, said, "Right, I'm off to lunch. I'll see you later. Good day, Dr Arnold."

Left alone with him, I was overcome with shyness and confusion and, for once in my life, I was unable to think of a single thing to say. He didn't make any small talk but said very directly, "Have dinner with me tonight."

It wasn't a question; it wasn't even a request. It was more a statement. "Thank you," I said. "That would be lovely." He smiled again, and I thought how truly enchanting that smile was.

"If you like French food I believe there is a restaurant in Little London off East Street. Would that appeal?"

"I love French food!" Then because I was afraid he would offer to pick me up, and I didn't want him to see where I lived or to have to introduce him to my mother, I said, "Let's meet in The Old Cross in North Street. Perhaps we can have a drink first."

"Perfect; shall we say about 7:30?"

"Yes." My voice was husky and I cleared my throat. "Yes. Thank you; lovely." I suddenly realized I'd already said lovely, so added, "See you at 7:30."

I hoped I sounded confident and sophisticated, but I have a feeling I sounded hesitant and overwhelmed. He was no sooner out of the office than Amber and Enid stuck their heads round the door. "Well?" they both asked in unison.

Without any reticence, Amber recommended what I ought to wear (my white knee-length boots, and a black and white A-line dress, with a low neckline and floating sleeves). She seemed to have taken on the role of personal outfitter, but I was satisfied with my appearance. My mother said, "Have a lovely time, darling. I'm glad you are going out."

In The Old Cross I was stunned to find Amber at the bar chatting to Pedro, that evening's barman. I glared at her. She grinned back. "Just checking that you look OK... and you do. Don't worry; I am not here to cramp your style. I'm just off."

She disappeared a moment or two later. There was no sign of Jack and I wondered what I should do. Was it appropriate to buy myself a drink, or should I wait for him? I tried to think what I might have done in those pre-convent days. But even as I moved to the bar the door swung open and he came in. There was a brief lull in the conversation in the bar, as black men were not common in Chichester and he was not a small man who could disappear in the crowd.

This was my first date after eight years of relative seclusion; I felt I needed something to stiffen my nerves, so I asked for a whisky and soda. He had a pint, and we found a seat in a quiet corner. He chatted easily and told me about himself. He was a New Zealander, not a South African as I had first thought. He was at the end of an eight-month spell in the UK. I found myself relaxing and began to enjoy the evening. He was a delightful companion, interesting and amusing. His body language was contained; that of a man at ease with himself. The only discordant note was the glances that were cast in our direction, occasionally accompanied by a muttered remark, followed by laughter.

"Don't worry," he said when he saw my discomfort. "It's much worse at home." Just as he spoke, a young man came into the bar, his long fair hair in Rastafarian dreadlocks. Nobody batted an eyelid at the appearance of this shaggy youth. "You see," pointed out Jack, "things could be worse; you could be with him." We both burst out laughing.

At dinner we talked about our families and our interests. His father was Maori, his mother Indian, which accounted for the aquiline features. Rugby was his passion, he informed me, and he laughed at my partiality for football, though I didn't tell him that my knowledge had been honed in the confines of a convent. He was sympathetic about my mother in a clinical kind of way, assuring me she would get better. "After all," he insisted, "she was fine without you before; she'll be fine without you again." We had coffee, and with regret I felt the evening drawing to a close.

"I finish at St Richard's in two days…" He paused, and then taking my hand continued, "Come back to the residency with me."

So I did. Which was why I found myself, some hour and a half later, lying beside him, with my head on his chest and his hand in my hair. It had been a supremely happy experience. He was a tender and considerate lover and I felt neither regret nor shame. What Catholics call concupiscence – selfish human desire for a person or thing – had not been a part of my life for so long that I found it strangely compelling.

I refused his offer to get a taxi for me or to walk me home. I needed to think. I had been rendered speechless when he had asked me abruptly as I got dressed to go back with him to New Zealand. "I'm thirty-four years of age, and in ten years I want to be throwing a rugby ball about with a son, or even kicking a football for that matter. We could really get to know each other; you are my kind of girl, and you would have a good job; the country is wonderful. We might have a great future together."

"I can't. It's impossible. I've only just moved. I've got a brand new job. There's my mother. It's not," I insisted, "because you are black." I was close to tears and was afraid that he might think it was. "You are such a lovely man; I wouldn't care if you were *green*! But it's too sudden and I can't make a decision about that now. It might be different if you were staying, but my life is in turmoil as it is at the moment."

I was off duty the following day and when I was next on, Amber told me that during my absence he had come to the unit to say goodbye.

"Dorothy gave him a crocheted tie."

"I don't believe you!"

"No, she didn't; just joking. At least his early departure saved him from that." We both burst out laughing. "I know," she said. "You laugh lest you weep."

She was right. And so Jack Arnold passed out of my life. I hope he found a splendid, gorgeous wife, because he deserved one.

CHAPTER 5

Di and Dee, and a Revelation

Eventually, to my immense relief, my mother and I found a flat in Stockbridge Road. A little further out from the centre of town, it was still within walking distance of the hospital. It was a pleasant first-floor, two-bedroomed apartment, with sitting room, kitchen-diner and bathroom. We moved in immediately. My mother was still showing no sign of looking for a job and her sleep patterns were very erratic. But if she was wandering nocturnally, at least she wasn't disturbing me. I found that with more personal space, I was becoming more detached about her needs and wants, but I didn't feel very proud about this. I prayed both for her and for me, that we should find what we needed. My own social life was busy, which meant she was on her own more and more, particularly in the evenings. Although we went to Mass together on Sunday, if I was off duty, it was almost the only casual interaction we had.

In July the maternity unit acquired another midwife. Her name was Diana Mann and we became friends almost immediately. She was a local girl; her parents had a beautiful flat above a very exclusive and expensive dress shop in North Street that her mother managed. Diana, always known as Di, a few years younger than me, was a dynamic, breezy blonde, full of energy. She was highly organized and super-confident. Her proudest possession was her little green Morris Minor 1000. She scoffed at it, calling it a little old lady's car, but privately she adored it and drove it with immense panache, or as her mother said, less poetically, "like a bat out of hell".

Fond as she was of her parents, Di told me that she had no intention of spending evenings and weekends sitting down glumly with them watching television, and accordingly she was game for a drink or two after work, whatever time she finished. Looking for company, she pointed out that The Old Cross pub and restaurant was on my way home, "providing you come via North Street and don't slink off through Priory Park". This was my usual way home, avoiding the centre of the city.

Di was familiar with both the pub and its owners. The food had an excellent reputation, for the chef had come from the Caprice in London. Di had worked behind the bar and in the restaurant during holiday periods. At that time it was *the* place to drink in. Amber too was roped in for these evening forays. So we would have a drink or two in the bar after work and then sneak round to the restaurant entrance waiting for Pedro, Amber's "platonic" boyfriend, and Pedro's fellow waiters to finish work.

If it was the weekend, and we weren't on duty the following day, we would all drift back to their digs in Franklin Place or St Paul's Road, to sit and drink several bottles of really excellent burgundy that the lads had "lifted" from the cellars. I re-acquired a nicotine habit, and was smoking with enthusiasm. These were fun evenings, full of laughter and mild flirtation. The boys were friendly and easygoing. Sometimes, one of them, a quiet but smiling Italian called Lorenzo, would cook omelettes for us or, on one memorable occasion, paella. I felt I was really living the high life.

I was just beginning to think I'd got things reasonably sorted when I was brought cruelly back to reality. Coming home to the flat after work one evening, I found my mother dazed and incoherent, her pills spread around the bed like Smarties. She was unable to tell me how many she had taken. As she began to slip into unconsciousness she mumbled that all she wanted was a good sleep. It was very fortunate that Di was with me and there was a public phone box on the corner. Leaving Di with her, I phoned the hospital and spoke to the Casualty doctor.

"Does she *have* to come in? I am a nurse; perhaps I can sort this out right here." I was distraught, and foolishly thought he might be able to give me advice that would allow me to deal with this crisis at home.

"You know she'll have to come in, don't you?" He was sympathetic but firm. "Even if you knew how many she had taken, she'd still need to be seen and treated. I'll send an ambulance for her." It came very quickly and she was whisked away to A&E. I felt a terrible mixture of pain and anger. I was too overwhelmed to cry.

"I don't want this." Sitting with Di in the kitchen over a cup of tea, I said, "I don't want to have to take care of my mother. If anything, I want somebody to take care of me."

"No, you don't. You just want a normal life. The sort of life you had perhaps when you were in Liverpool," pointed out Di. She sounded hesitant and looked at me quizzically. She was startled by my almost hysterical laughter. If only she knew. "What? What have I said?" she demanded. I couldn't answer her.

That moment was the first and only time I genuinely felt regret and remorse about leaving my convent. Just for a brief moment I longed for Mary-Mount and the reassuring familiarity and comfort of my community. My tears when they came were for my past life, not my poor mother.

When I went to bring her home, the ever-supportive Di came with me and we drove my mother back to the flat. I didn't know what to say to her and she was equally taciturn. She accepted her night-time pills with good grace, even when I told her I was keeping them. The following morning she was pleasant, if a little cool, at breakfast and said she had had a good night. She was out when I got home.

A little later she arrived, to my surprise, with our landlord from the previous lodgings. She announced calmly but determinedly that she was moving back there. He had offered her accommodation, and she felt it best if we lived independently. I hope she didn't see the relief on my face, but I fear she did, as she said with some bitterness, "Actually, it's you who should be going." When I pointed out that the rent of the flat was beyond her financial means, she said, "How will you manage?" and I had to acknowledge that I didn't know.

She packed up her few belongings, turning down my offer to

help. Her landlord waited in his car, and Di and I sat in silence in the sitting room.

"I'll come round and make sure you have all you need tomorrow," I said, as I saw her to the car.

"Thank you," she replied colourlessly. Her disappointment about the failure of our experimental communal living was tangible.

I went slowly indoors feeling miserable about the whole thing. Back in the sitting room I found Di looking thoughtfully out of the window. Turning to me she grimaced sympathetically.

"If you are looking for a flatmate, someone to split the rent with, I wouldn't mind moving in," she said hesitantly. "If you don't think I'm pushing it a bit."

I felt a rush of relief, and pleasure. Nothing could have pleased me more.

"Good God, that would be wonderful! But what about your parents? Won't they kick up a fuss?"

"Oh yes, I expect so, on principle probably. But I think, in their heart of hearts, they'll be pleased to be rid of me. Their flat is nice but it is quite small." Then ever practical and cool-headed she continued, "Think it over. We'll talk about it, perhaps tomorrow evening."

We drove out to a pub near Bosham the next evening and went into the bar.

"Why do you always drink shorts?" she enquired, not without irritation. "They are terribly expensive."

"I haven't much experience of beer."

"They sell great stuff here. It's called Director's ale. Try it. It's what I am having."

Over a glass of Director's we discussed her moving into Stockbridge Road and came to a very happy agreement. The idea of having a companion of my own age, and one that was such fun, filled me with exhilaration. After two further half pints of Director's, I was, I thought, light-headed with relief. In the ladies loo, I missed my step and sprawled full length on the floor, where I lay dazed for a moment or two before sitting up and promptly bashing my head on the washbasin. Di found me about five minutes later and hauled me to my feet. I stood swaying, as the room revolved around me.

"Honestly," she said in a disbelieving voice, "I watched you crossing the floor. You really can't hold your liquor, can you?" A rhetorical question if ever I heard one. "Let's get you out of here. I think they've got a new carpet, so whatever you do, don't puke in the bar... Or in my car either, which would be much worse!"

I felt dreadful next morning, not only from the thundering headache but from a sense of shame. Being a little happy on two glasses of Babycham in a convent, where only the community might notice a pink nose and flushed cheeks, was a bit different from getting legless in a public bar.

Di moved into Stockbridge Road about a week later, and about a week after that Amber told us that a nurse who worked in the main hospital was also looking for somewhere to live in the town. We talked about it over coffee and decided it would be an advantage to have a third flatmate. Di's bedroom had a single bed but mine had a double. If she didn't mind sharing, then it might be feasible.

We arranged to meet, as ever, in The Old Cross. Dee was a slender, pretty girl with pale skin and silky dark hair cut in a bob. Her quietness, and what seemed at first like reserve, made me question how she would fit in with ebullient Di and gabby me, but we needn't have worried. She turned out to have a wicked sense of humour and be so quick-witted that within a very short time we were pressing her to move in as soon as she could. The double bed issue was quickly resolved, Dee stating that I could sleep on the floor or we could take it in turns! This was said with such a straight face that for a moment we were aghast, but then she laughed and pointed out that as we all had different night duty rotas there would be wonderful times when we actually had a bed to ourselves. On all other occasions she was sure we would adapt. We knew we had found a kindred spirit.

When she recommended Dee to us, it was almost the last time we talked to Amber; she was working her notice and a fortnight or so later returned to Belfast and presumably to her fiancé. Pedro took her departure with cheerful equanimity, as far as we could tell.

My mother had settled back into a smaller room in our old digs. She seemed contented enough. She had found a couple of second-hand bookshops that seemed, she informed me, to be promising. She preferred going to an evening Mass on Saturday, so our interaction became even more infrequent. I was concerned about her but not overly worried.

At Stockbridge Road life was cheerful and companionable. If we were all off duty together Di was invariably full of plans for what we might do. One evening we went to Brighton, to the Silver Blades ice rink. Both Di and Dee had been before and had mastered the art of staying upright on ice-skates. It appeared deceptively easy and so attractive. The music and the lights and the sinuous figures on the ice looked enchanting.

Ever confident, I was sure I would master it. It couldn't be harder than roller-skating and I'd done plenty of that as a girl. But once on the ice, I was like Bambi, legs and arms in every direction, and more often than not on my backside. I seemed to have no control at all over my feet, which had independent lives of their own and felt completely detached from my legs. I clung grimly to the rail.

"Strike out," shouted Dee encouragingly, zipping past.

Di skidded to a halt beside me. "You've got to keep moving forward. You can't skate standing still!" She linked arms with me. "Right foot, left foot, push and glide, push and glide."

Suddenly I was skating. "I've got it, I've got it," I yelled, striking out boldly and as it transpired foolhardily. I shot out into the throng and was then jostled by a dashing skater with tight jeans and a total lack of consideration for the debutants on the rink. I crashed into the barrier and was on my backside again.

"Ice hog!" shouted Di after him.

We stopped as usual at a pub on the way home. It seems incredible now, but in the sixties and seventies, before the advent of severe penalties for driving while over the limit, people thought nothing of drinking several beers or whatever alcoholic beverage they preferred, and then driving home. It would have been considered positively "wimpish" to have called for a taxi or to have refused a drink on the grounds of needing to drive home. Indeed the encouragement to have "one for the road" was commonplace. It would have been more exact to have recommended "one for the ditch".

We arrived home safely, and having had such an excellent evening decided to open a bottle of wine and have a night-cap. Sitting at the kitchen table, relaxed and happy, I was suddenly smitten with an overwhelming desire to tell these lovely new friends, my flatmates, about my past life; a life I had kept a secret from everyone, apart from Stuart whom I had come upon unexpectedly, since leaving Liverpool.

"Listen," I announced, "there is something I want to tell you. About my past; about what I've been doing for the last eight years."

They looked at me in some consternation. Di refilled our glasses. There was a long silence.

"OK," said Dee.

"Go on then," said Di.

I took a deep breath. "I was a nun; three and a half years in France as a novice, and then a nun in Liverpool. I did my training as a nurse and midwife as a nun."

They looked at each other for a moment and then Di said, "Thank God you've told us! We thought you'd been in prison!"

"In *prison*? Why on earth did you think I'd been in prison?"

"Because you didn't know *anything*: not the price of clothes, or fags or drinks or anything. What twenty-six-year-old in regular employment doesn't have a bank account nor know how to write a cheque? You don't know any of the pop songs – well, except for those by the Beatles. You haven't seen any recent films apart from *Rosemary's Baby*. You don't seem to have read anything except the classics. You are completely ignorant about modern life. We have been trying to think what you could have done that was so bad that you were banged up for eight years."

"All has now been made clear," said Dee. "Obviously we are going to have to take you in hand."

And to my eternal gratitude that's just what they did.

CHAPTER 6

Tales from the Unit

Chichester, I discovered, had a lot going for it. An enchanting Georgian town built on Roman foundations, it was smaller and more intimate than either Winchester or Salisbury, the other cathedral cities nearby. The cathedral itself, situated in the very centre of town, paled beside Winchester's gothic magnificence and Salisbury's soaring elegance. But although architecturally more modest than its rivals, it was in fact the oldest of the three and I always felt it had a comfortable, domestic quality about it. It was sober and dignified. I felt at home in its cool and calm interior, and would go in occasionally for a few minutes of peace and quiet, wandering down the nave and the side aisles, soothed by the silent monumental tombs peacefully covering long-dead forebears. Coming out through the cloister, with its beautiful wooden roof, I would go into the Crypt café and drink hot chocolate and eat toasted teacakes.

The city's other main attraction was the Festival theatre, which stood in the middle of a pleasant park. The summer season ran for three months and attracted nationally recognized figures, both actors and directors. It had a reputation for presenting avant-garde as well as traditional productions. It was quite common to see the glitterati in the bar of The Old Cross. Patricia Routledge, Maggie Smith and Alastair Sim rubbed shoulders happily with the locals, but Laurence Harvey, startling in shocking pink overalls, was very aloof.

"He can't help his height," said Dee, in response to my comment that he seemed to find everybody beneath his notice. "We're all beneath his nose, if not his notice. He must be well over six foot tall and lean as a whippet."

Dora Bryan, another regular, was charming; she once bought a round of drinks for the entire pub, and was very bawdy, in a jolly sort of way. She seemed oblivious to the effect her loud expletives were having on the rest of the drinkers, who tut-tutted into their G and Ts but never refused her offer of a drink.

A huge attraction in the area was the proximity of Chichester Harbour, a large and irregular body of water linking three other harbours: Portsmouth, Langstone and Pagham. It was extremely pretty with willow-lined creeks and a huge variety of birds, both native and migratory. It was demanding for all but the most competent sailors, being deep, with a swift tidal flow near the entrance, and extremely shallow in other areas with numerous sand bars. Knowledge of the tides was essential, otherwise a boat could find itself beached on a mudflat with all the attendant inconvenience.

This was demonstrated to me very clearly one beautiful summer morning at about 6 a.m. I was on night duty, when I took a call from the ambulance depot. They were bringing in a girl from Dell Quay, a little village on the harbour. She was in strong labour but only thirty-four weeks pregnant. The switchboard girl added, "She's very dirty, I'm told; you'll need a hose-pipe. She's not booked in to you, so you won't have the notes. A Londoner, I think. Her husband's with her."

I went to get the labour room ready, a bit irritated as I realized that I would be delayed getting off duty. Dorothy, who had been on with me that night, was busy delivering another baby, so I stuck my head round the door to tell her what was happening, and then ran a bath, thinking this would be the best way to deal with dirt. The girl arrived wrapped in a filthy blanket. Her husband was quiet and pale but the girl was cheerful and giggly.

They had come down the previous evening for a weekend sailing. When her contractions woke her at 5 a.m. on Saturday, she was stunned to discover that the boat was high and dry on the mud. There was nothing for it but to stagger ashore as best they could.

Clinging to each other, ploughing through the thick, greasy black slime had taken a Herculean effort. She told me that at one point she had feared they would never make it, and resorted to shouting for help. They were both in mud up to their thighs, but had had the foresight to bring the dinghy oars with them, which gave them some purchase. Eventually they reached the pub, and the friendly landlord, appalled at the sight of them and at the ghastly thought that the girl might have given birth in the mud, phoned immediately for the ambulance.

It took two full tubs of water to get her clean, and even then her feet and nails were grimed. "You look like the creature from the black lagoon," I told her. Her husband sat with her for a while and then went outside to have a cigarette and calm his nerves.

Her labour progressed normally and she chatted about herself and her family. She had been well throughout the pregnancy, but was a little concerned about the unexpected and premature onset of her labour, as was I, although all seemed well. When she began second stage she pushed determinedly, chattering all the time between pushes. After about ten minutes, which surprised me as second stage can be prolonged, particularly with a first baby, she was delivered of a small but perfectly healthy boy. I cut the cord and wrapped the infant up in a towel for her to hold. When I put my hand on her abdomen to feel her uterus I realized immediately that there was another foetus there. I said nothing for a moment but listened to the baby's heart, which was strong and steady. I just looked at my patient and smiled.

"Oh," she wrinkled her nose. "I'm still getting contractions."

"That's because you have another one in there."

The second baby was born about fifteen minutes later, slightly smaller but still healthy; this time a little girl. My patient was ecstatic.

"We thought of Reuben for a boy or Rachel for a girl. Now we can have both."

"Whatever next! A good Jewish girl like you, sailing on the sabbath," I teased her.

"We are Reform Jews," she said. "I think it's OK." Then she

added, "Don't tell my husband it's twins. I want to surprise him."

Her husband had regained some colour in his cheeks, but not for long. He arrived, proudly smiling, and as he bent to kiss her, saw not one but two bundles. He cast a startled look at me, blenched again and sank unconscious to the floor.

Dorothy, who arrived to take the babies, recommended leaving him to come round on his own. Sure enough after a minute or two he staggered to his feet and sat down shakily next to his wife. "Twins," he kept repeating. "Twins!"

This episode, which ended happily, nevertheless characterized one of the difficulties we had delivering women who were not booked in with us. We had limited knowledge of their obstetric history, and prior to the advent of scans, which these days are often carried around proudly by expectant mothers, we frequently had no idea what we were getting.

On another occasion the baby's head began to emerge with what looked like a large tumour on it. I pressed the buzzer and Di came in to help. We stared aghast at the growth that appeared at the vulva every time our patient pushed. Di went quietly and quickly to ring for the duty doctor. He arrived promptly, and bent down to examine the presenting part. He looked up grinning, "Good God, girls, haven't you seen testicles before? It's a breech. Get me some gloves."

In the summer Chichester became quite a cosmopolitan society. West Sussex is a delightful county, and away from the water the landscape of rolling downland, interspersed with picturesque villages and charming little towns, brought a great influx of tourists, attracted by the architecture and the delightful rural environment. The theatrical world, both actors and the supporting crew, filled the pubs and restaurants. Many rented flats or houses for the duration of the summer festival. Some brought their families, and a pregnant wife or girlfriend would book into the antenatal clinic rather than return home, in order to be registered with us in case of going into labour unexpectedly. Di delivered the wife of a well-known and recognized actor, and the glory rubbed off on all of us. She said he was delightful. We received a huge box of chocolates, the usual but unimaginative "thank you". Di said she would have preferred a free theatre ticket.

Some of the girls that came in from the outlying villages were a delight. They had a freshness and relaxed attitude even with a first baby, and rarely suffered any of the serious complications that can arise. Dee was of the opinion that they had seen so many pigs, sheep and cows give birth they were pretty sanguine about their own delivery. Certainly very few came into the unit before their waters broke, and many continued whatever work they were doing until they weren't far off second stage. Some left it too late and were delivered in the ambulance or even in the farm pick-up truck.

One girl's husband phoned in to say she would come in when she'd finished strawberry picking. She arrived several hours later, sun-browned and still in her work clothes. Her feet and legs were dusty and she smelled of strawberries, her lips stained with juice. It was her first baby, and the notes indicated she had had a trouble-free pregnancy. Her contractions were about every five minutes. Her blood pressure was quite normal and the foetal heart strong and regular. As her waters were intact and she was sweaty and grubby, I decided to wait until she had bathed before doing an internal examination. I ran a bath, helped her in and sat on the rim chatting to her. Every so often she would give a little grunt and when I put my hand on her abdomen, I felt the uterus contracting.

"Let's get you out," I said, "and see what's happening."

As I was drying her back she gave another little grunt, then laughed. "I've got a sort of burning feeling between my legs," she announced.

I dropped to my knees and peered up at her crotch. The baby's head had almost crowned! I put my hand between her legs to hold it back and said, "Just breathe. No pushing." Then I frogmarched her into the labour ward, heaved her up onto the bed and five minutes later was cutting the cord. It was a perfect delivery; and she didn't even tear. I don't believe she suffered a single moment of pain.

"Serves you right," said Sister Baines. "She could have had that baby in the bath. You should have done a vaginal when she came in."

"Water births are the coming thing," said Enid, placatingly. She was sorting some filing and grimaced sympathetically at me.

"Not in my unit, they're not!" said Baines.

My country girl went home, and a week later her husband brought in two large crates of strawberries. We gorged on them for days.

Not all deliveries were straightforward, however, and some mothers suffered the anguish of labouring to bring a dead infant into the world. We sent them home as early as we could, but if they had had a forceps delivery or a caesarean section, they had to remain for longer. We kept them in a side room, so they were not subjected to the sight of contented mothers nursing their thriving babies. It was particularly hard if expectations were dashed. One charming girl, a severe diabetic, had lost her first child late in pregnancy, a not uncommon event for women suffering from that condition. With her second pregnancy she was registered for a planned caesarean. When she came into the unit we couldn't hear the foetal heart. She refused to believe the registrar when he broke the news gently to her and she insisted she could feel the baby moving.

"This one is quite different," she assured him. "I've carried it differently; it just feels fine."

We knew the baby was very large. There was no question of a normal delivery. So she had her caesarean. The dead infant was huge and bloated, and it was a struggle even to deliver it surgically.

"Oh God," said one of the other midwives, wrapping the sad corpse in a towel. "I just hope she doesn't want to see it."

Once I delivered a baby of about twenty weeks' gestation. The mother was admitted in labour. The foetal heart was audible and the baby was still moving, so she came to the maternity unit rather than the gynae ward. As the tiny infant slid almost effortlessly out, I saw it was still enclosed in the amniotic sac. It was about six inches long and it fitted into a kidney dish. To my horror I saw its fairy-like limbs were moving. I gazed at it, appalled. It had absolutely no prospect of life.

"Take it into the sluice," Sister Baines said quietly.

In the sluice, I saw it had stopped moving. I ran a little water into a jug, then very carefully I tore the amniotic sac, poured the water onto the tiny head and whispered the words of baptism. Then I covered the dish and went back into the labour room. On my way back home that evening I slipped into St Richard's Church and thought of that perfectly formed body and prayed that, like David, the dying baby I had nursed in Liverpool, this one too was now whole and perfect.

Very occasionally, we had a maternal death. Although very uncommon, it did occur. This was dreadful for everybody. Mothers were not expected to die, childbirth being a natural process. But patients with any serious underlying health problems were always at risk, as were women who developed high blood pressure due to pre-eclampsia. If amniotic fluid or waste products found their way into the maternal bloodstream following delivery, and caused an embolus, a woman could collapse suddenly and die with horrifying rapidity. Sudden, violent haemorrhages were not unknown. Thankfully, due to the advent of antibiotics and antiseptic procedures, the dreadful puerperal fever that claimed so many, even in the early twentieth century, had been vanquished from maternity units, but eclampsia still haunted us.

As the summer drifted into autumn, my sense of security and independence grew. I felt at ease and my friends were supportive. My mother seemed settled and I saw her regularly, usually a couple of times a week.

Once I had bared my soul about my past to Di and Dee there seemed no reason to keep it secret. It wasn't a matter of revelation – more the fact of saying in all simplicity, when asked, that I hadn't gone to nightclubs in Liverpool because I had been living in a religious community. Few people seemed embarrassed about my past; most were curious, and almost all were mystified. The recurrent question was, "Why? Whatever made you do it?" I tended to get tongue-tied. I didn't think people wanted to hear about giving up everything for God, or my conviction that I had been called to the life. The concept of a religious vocation is extraordinarily difficult to put into words, so I wasn't very brave about trying to explain it. I wasn't ashamed of it. I just didn't want to appear odd or different. I wanted to fit in, to drink and smoke and to chat up the boys as the others were doing, so I tried very hard to avoid situations where I might be constrained to explain.

There were things I was still getting to grips with. I had no idea what "flower power" meant. I thought a commune sounded great; hadn't I just lived in one? I wasn't sure about "hippies" – what was all that long hair about? I thought the multi-coloured patchwork jeans lovely; were they psychedelic? What did that mean? A "trip" sounded fun. Where did people go? Why was it so risky? The Bee Gees and the Beach Boys were strangers to me, although I did know Cilla Black; as a Liver bird, she was accepted in Mary-Mount. Woodstock, for me, was a pretty town in Oxfordshire, and wasn't "love" free anyway? I didn't ask too many questions. I didn't want to appear naïve or ignorant, although in fact I was both.

The faux sophistication that I had been so proud of when I was seventeen or eighteen was not much help to me aged twenty-six. In fact, my lack of worldliness contributed to some unfortunate experiences. Jack Arnold had been honest and direct, but many men were more devious. At a party in the nurses' home I met a very good-looking and delightfully friendly young man who asked me out for a drink. He was suave and elegant, an educated man. I thought he might have been in the services, the army perhaps. He was amusing and chatty in the pub the following day and I liked the look of him. I asked him where he lived. He replied that he lived with his parents. I was startled that such a man should not have a house of his own. He saw the expression of surprise on my face and misread it; he reddened. "No," he said, smiling brazenly, despite his blush. "I'm married. You know that I'm married. Of course you do."

I was dumbfounded and suddenly blazingly angry. "How should I know that you're married? You were at a party, behaving like a single man. You're not wearing a ring. You ask me out, as if you are free. How am I supposed to know that you are married? Does your wife know that you are out on the pull?" This vulgar expression I had heard quite recently and although I found it vaguely repellent I thought it suited the situation exactly.

"I'm sorry," he said, inadequately.

I banged my unfinished drink down and left the bar.

"Put it down to experience," said Dee.

"And don't ask them in for coffee," said Di, after the second or third instance when I felt I had had to fight for my virtue (such as it was), after what had been a really lovely evening. A simple goodnight kiss didn't seem to be what they had on their minds once ensconced on the sofa. My comment that I thought it a pleasant way to end the evening brought forth laughter from Dee and exasperated sighs from Di.

"Inviting them in for coffee doesn't signal the end of the evening. More like the beginning of the rest of it."

CHAPTER 7

A Seriously Foolish Affair

In The Old Cross one night, there was an extraordinarily good-looking young man behind the bar, someone I hadn't seen before. Lorenzo, one of the waiters, stuck his head round the corner of the restaurant, and seeing us there popped across quickly to say hello to Dee. It was evident that he was becoming more than a little interested in her.

"Oh him!" he said dismissively, in response to my query. "That's Philippe. He's just back from Switzerland."

Lorenzo's lack of enthusiasm, I felt, was more to do with wanting to talk Philippe down than any real antagonism. He certainly didn't want Dee to be drawn to this new and undeniably attractive figure.

Philippe was not just handsome, although he was certainly that. He had real charm, "charisma even", as Dee said later. Although not above average height, he would have attracted attention anywhere. His astonishing good looks were less in the perfect symmetry of his features, the smooth olive skin, the sleek dark hair, the fit muscular frame, the beautiful teeth, the dazzling smile, than in the overall impression he gave of being easy, relaxed and happy to be who he was. He exuded a pleasant self-confidence together with undeniable sex appeal. If ever a man knew he was irresistible it was Philippe. Yet he was neither boastful nor arrogant; rather, good-natured and easy going. His smile was sweet. Unsurprisingly he was popular with his employers and the other waiters, and a magnet for the girls. I thought he looked wonderful.

I saw him several times, either in the pub, or from a distance, around town. Chichester was not very big but I never seemed to have the opportunity to meet him properly. Eventually, inevitably, carrying the expected bottle of wine, he turned up at Pedro's house one evening, where a little group of us were gathered. Philippe, I discovered, always had an eye for a new face. He came straight across to sit beside me and began to chat. I saw the knowing grins on the others' faces and I felt flustered. His very proximity was disturbing. He came from a French-speaking canton in Switzerland, so a big attraction, for both of us, was that we could speak French together. He was beguilingly flirtatious but not pushy.

We met regularly in the evenings, always with other people. He had digs in the city. He drove a battered old Ford with terrifying recklessness. Unsurprisingly, given his behaviour behind the wheel, his own car, a Mini Cooper, was in a repair garage in Portsmouth. He had been in a collision with a petrol tanker. He was lucky not to have been killed. Petrol tankers are very large and Mini Coopers very... well, mini.

One Saturday afternoon we drove out to the garage, a hanger on the industrial estate growing up on the old Portsmouth airfield, to see how the repair work was progressing. It was shut. He tried to scramble up to peer through the high windows but couldn't manage it, so he lifted me up to have a look. I failed to identify his little car among the huge pile of wrecks piled on top of each other, so he let me down. I turned in the circle of his arms and was opening my mouth to ask him if they really were going to repair it, when he kissed me.

He had kissed me before, the usual kiss on the cheek so common in France, but this was different. When the kiss was finished he didn't speak, but smiled quizzically. Then he took my hand and began to lead me back to the old car. Just before we reached it, he bent and picked a large dandelion. He handed it to me with another smile and said, "*Une fleur pour mademoiselle.*" I thought, stupidly and very unwisely, I'm in love. I wasn't, but I certainly wanted him very badly; "badly" being the operative word.

I spent the night with him, then had to leave very early in order to get back home to change into my uniform, ready to be on duty at 7:30 a.m. He ran me back to Stockbridge Road, got out of the car and kissed me sweetly, then gently turned my hand and kissed the palm. He didn't speak, and some element of common sense prevented me from asking when I would see him again.

"*Bisou, chéri*," I said with the same irony that he had used when he presented me with the dandelion.

Then he laughed and pulled me against him, saying, "*À ce soir*."

Back at the flat, Di was still in bed but Dee was making breakfast. "You see," she said. "I told you there would be nights when we'd have the bed to ourselves." As I left the flat I saw Lorenzo's car parked in the side road.

Then began a strange time in my life. I can't say I felt guilty or regretful. I was so enthralled by this man that there didn't seem any space for shame or any awareness of betraying my Catholic principles. I thought vaguely about the risk of pregnancy and eventually went to see my GP, my local doctor, about contraception. I didn't feel guilty about that either. It was as if I was living in an altogether different world where I wasn't Eleanor, a good Catholic, an ex-nun, who lived according to the tenets of her faith, but Eleanor the wild child, the modern young woman, controlling her own life, making her own choices; free!

It was all nonsense. I wasn't in love at all. I suppose it was lust, although truth to tell, Philippe, for all his beauty, was not a particularly wonderful bed mate. He was always affectionate and certainly seductive to look at, but I was often left with the impression that he wanted to get it over with as quickly as possible. He wasn't selfish or impatient, just business-like, so there wasn't always a great deal of satisfaction in it for me, who was looking, above all, for romance. For all his sweetness of temperament – I never heard him be unkind or harsh to anyone – there was not a great deal of depth in Philippe. Compared to Lorenzo, who was considerate and thoughtful with others, and loving and caring with Dee, my chap was a bit of a lightweight. He was perfectly honest – he never pretended he loved me, nor that I was more important than any other girl, and I suspected that there were others. Yet when I was with him I felt cocooned in a private bubble of specialness. A day without seeing him was desolation. An ex-lover of his, who had morphed into a good friend, warned me: "Be careful. He's lovely, I know, but he has had a lot of partners." Philippe himself, on more than one occasion, told me, "You are too good for me. You should find yourself a nice boy who will love and take care of you. I'm not really right for you." He was quite correct, but I was deaf to it all.

He would sometimes come to the flat after work, occasionally after we had all gone to bed. He always accepted with cheerfulness that the only thing I could offer him was a cup of coffee or a glass of wine. "Dee's asleep and I'm not rolling around on the floor – not even for you," I told him, and he grinned.

Conveniently, Di, Dee and I made a discovery that proved very useful. On the landing was a flight of stairs leading to an attic, the use of which was not included in our rental agreement. One day we climbed up, pushed open the trap door and discovered a sizable room with a bed in it. We made use of it whenever the necessity arose.

This disregard for the verbal agreement that constituted our lease possibly contributed to our landlord's unexpected decision to give us notice when we had been in the flat barely three months. We were stunned, particularly as we had just finished painting the kitchen. The Citizens Advice Bureau recommended that we appeal, which we did, and were given a year's security of tenure, which we thought would be adequate. Di and I were sure we wouldn't be staying in Chichester for ever. We weren't too sure about Dee, who seemed happy to stay on at St Richard's. We celebrated our victory over our landlord by throwing a party. It was a riotous evening and eventually we fell into bed about 3 a.m.

I woke to hear a thunderous knocking on the door and, looking blearily at my watch, saw it was about 6 a.m.

"If it's the police," said Di, struggling into her dressing gown as I went to the door, "tell them they have missed the party!"

It wasn't the police. It was my mother's landlord. "Your mum's had an accident," he said. She had bought a little butane gas ring for cooking on. It was against the rules of the house but she did it anyway, and her landlord turned a blind eye. She was smoking while changing the cylinder and either didn't fasten it properly or the old one was not fully empty. There was a huge explosion and her legs were badly burnt. She was in hospital. Yet again I was flooded with guilt and anguish.

We found her bandaged and heavily sedated. I was overwhelmed at how small and fragile she looked. I sat by her bed holding her hand. I was told she would need skin grafts but was not in any danger. It was small comfort.

Di drove me into Portsmouth to talk to my brother, Peter. He was shaken and dismayed. "What are we going to do with her?" he asked.

"At the moment, we don't need to do anything. She's probably going to be in hospital for some weeks. But we've got to sort out something. I love her very much, but I cannot live with her again."

We drove back home. Di was very quiet and I was very depressed. At the maternity unit, my colleagues were supportive and when we weren't busy Sister Baines gave me time to go to see my mother in the afternoon. Philippe, softhearted and sympathetic, came with me occasionally if he wasn't working, and, typically, charmed her, chatting in French and telling her how lucky she was to have such a lovely daughter. sentiments I half agreed with but with some ambivalence, given our recent history. Peter came over several times with Linda his fiancée and they came back to the flat for baked potatoes and a glass of wine, but we were no closer to finding a solution.

Di's mother, Maxine, was also kind and attentive with cards and flowers. There was sometimes a briskness about Maxine that could be off-putting, but it could also galvanize people into action. So she asked my mother where she was going when she left hospital, and what she was going to do. This question had me quivering with anxiety. My mother replied firmly that she had had quite enough of Chichester, which had been, she pronounced, "very unlucky" for her. I was filled with relief. She didn't say exactly what she had planned, but she clearly intended an independent life.

"Perhaps she'll go back to Scotland," suggested Dee.

"Oh, if only," I groaned.

I was astonished at the speed with which she recovered. All the skin grafts were successful, and although the areas of flayed flesh on her thighs from where the skin had been taken looked livid, they healed rapidly. She spent Christmas in hospital and said she had had a truly lovely time. "The nurses sang carols. Those girls are wonderful; I can find no fault with them." Then she added, "Although the Coventry Carol was dreadfully badly sung."

"It's composed in a minor key, Mummy, so some people find it odd."

"That's an interesting argument to put forward for singing out of tune," she replied tersely.

I spent Christmas morning with her and thought she looked better than I had seen her since I'd come home.

She was in hospital for barely a month and then went to a convalescent home near the village of Liss. Di ran me out there several times to see her.

"Do you know what they told me?" my mother announced indignantly when we went to visit. "They told me I must resign myself to walking with a stick. I told them I would never, ever walk with a stick." She was quite determined, and even when very old she never ever used one.

After about ten days in the convalescent home she was invited by Linda's parents to stay with them in their Brighton home. Almost miraculously, this appalling accident that could have killed her was the catalyst for the transformation of her life. She found a pleasant little studio flat in Hove and set about looking for a job. Eventually she found one that suited her perfectly. She became the office manager for a small estate agent dealing in commercial properties.

"It's wonderful," she told me. "I feel like a new woman." She looked it too. The drawn, anguished look had gone, to be replaced by a cheerful smiling face. I had not seen her like that since before I entered my convent. Our relationship, recently so difficult and unsatisfactory, became relaxed and affectionate.

Di, Dee and I had a hilarious Christmas at Stockbridge Road. Lorenzo joined us and supervised the cooking. I think roast turkey mystified him, but he was an enthusiast for Christmas pudding. He had a very sweet tooth and loved all puddings, his favourite being apple crumble, which he called "scrambled pie". His attachment to Dee was clearly very strong and we knew that it was reciprocated.

One evening, sitting on the stairs, she told us she was pregnant. She was bemused but wonderfully happy and terribly excited. We were happy for her.

My relationship with Philippe, if I can call it such, drifted on. Happy when I was with him, I was not so much unhappy as dissatisfied when I wasn't with him. I wondered, in my rational moments, why on earth I was wasting my time.

"You know he's just taking advantage of you, stringing you along, don't you?" said Di. She had been surprisingly uncritical of the whole thing, as she too was aware of Philippe's allure, but she saw the situation clearly and recognized the inevitability of the outcome.

"I'm afraid I agree," said Dee. "I know he's charming, but Lorenzo says he's seeing another girl."

I think they had both decided that I had to face the truth. Di continued, "Charm is what he is. He's even charmed my mother, who keeps telling me that he's a lovely boy!" Di's mother, lunching in The Old Cross, had spilled something on her dress and Philippe had rushed to remedy the situation.

"He sponged it down so neatly," she said.

"Any excuse to get his hand up a skirt," Di said sourly.

I began to cool the whole scenario. We slipped into affectionate but non-sexual friendship. It says a great deal about Philippe's nature that this was what usually happened with his ex-partners. There were moments when he smiled at me or I saw him smile the same way at others and I felt a wrench so all-encompassing that I had to turn away to hide my prickling eyes, but in the end I mastered it. Stepping back, I was even able to see defects in his physical perfection. Once, when we'd all gone to the beach, Philippe and Pedro were standing close by smoking and attracting more than their fair share of attention. Dee said to me, "Have you noticed Philippe is ever so slightly knock-kneed?" Although I hotly refuted it, as I sat up and peered at him, on closer examination I had to admit it was true. "Yes. My God, you're right. I've never noticed."

"You wouldn't," she said. "I don't suppose he did much standing up when you were alone together!"

Then the situation was resolved for me. Philippe told me he was returning to Switzerland to work with his uncle. "You'll find someone better than me," he said. I cried a little and felt wretched for a day or two, but deep down there was a feeling of relief. Nearly a year of such high emotion, either with my mother or with Philippe, had left me drained, and I looked forward to a more peaceful time. The whole episode should have instilled, if not some sense or moderation, at least some caution in me, but it didn't.

CHAPTER 8

Penzance and the Lure of Crayfish

"Do you fancy a trip to Penzance?"

Here was another of Di's "let's go for it" moments, so I accepted with alacrity. A friend of hers, a girl called Marcia, had invited her to stay and kindly included me. We both had Friday off and planned to set off early. It did occur to me that February is not the best time of year for a trip to the West Country, or indeed anywhere in the northern hemisphere. The weather forecast predicted snow and there was an icy wind. As I didn't drive, the possible ramifications of what amounted to a major expedition in an old car passed over my head. It was a long journey in those pre-motorway days. Di estimated about five hours but agreed this was probably optimistic.

The countryside was ravishingly beautiful. A heavy hoar frost covered the land in the morning, coating the pasture and the trees like icing sugar. When the sun was high the dripping and the melting glistened and sparkled. The sky looked newly washed and was a pale delicate blue. The heater in the car was erratic, so we had wrapped up as if for a trek to the South Pole. We spent the entire day wrapping and then unwrapping ourselves as the heater alternately blew hothouse warm and arctic cold. The journey seemed interminable, but Di was, as ever, good company. We chatted and laughed, I obeying the frequent directive of "Flash the ash, then", which was a signal to light up.

We had arranged a rendezvous with Marcia and her partner

Felix, in a flat they were renting in Penzance. We arrived before dark and found the place without too much difficulty. The welcome was friendly, if casual. There seemed to be a considerable number of people wandering in and out, equally friendly. We were stunned to discover that Di's friends were moving house that very evening. It seemed an extraordinary thing to do. You tend not to have people to stay the day you move house. Doing both at the same time struck me as more than a little eccentric. It occurred to me that perhaps they were looking for extra muscle, but I did them an injustice. All that was left to move was a basket of none-too-clean-looking linen, some curious and heavy equipment, including a scuba mask and some fins, and, of all things, a large and smelly lobster pot.

We were not offered a cup of tea but an alcoholic drink, so after over six hours' travel, with very little to eat except a sandwich Dee had made for us and we had eaten before 10 o'clock, we found ourselves with a large mug ("The glasses are packed, I'm afraid") of the favoured drink of the time, a rough red Valpolicella.

It tasted very good, and I was filled with warmth and an ever so slightly reckless idea that, here, I was going to make a whole new circle of friends. I examined the group covertly. The atmosphere was, I decided, bohemian. The people were charming, friendly and in the main well spoken and had, I thought, the unconsciously superior and confident manner of the privately educated. And yet it was difficult to categorize them. There was a certain uniformity about them, the men wearing fishermen's smocks, shoddy and worn, or Guernsey jumpers, one or two holed at the elbow. Their hair was longish, their jeans scruffy; several were barefooted. The three girls, Marcia included, wore huge outsized jumpers and floaty skirts. I couldn't imagine what they did for a living.

We were on our second "glass" of wine when unexpectedly everyone sat down to watch *Top of the Pops*. Someone behind me said, "See the dark-haired girl on the left? I love the way her breasts sway in that dress." There was a little murmur of agreement; I have to say, not only from the men. I had always felt that Pan's People were pretty lumpy dancers, but the boldness of the statement and the ease with which it was made and the calmness of the reaction stunned me. I caught sight of the speaker behind me, a fair-haired man with a tanned face and deep lines from nose to mouth. His age was intriguingly indeterminate. He could have been anything between twenty-five and forty. He grinned at me and raised an eyebrow.

Marcia and Felix's new flat was in Marazion, only a short distance around the bay from Penzance. It was large and elegant, but bitterly cold. We got a fire going, which took the chill off the room, and more alcohol warmed me up. I began to learn about the curious, and to my mind exotic, lifestyle in which these new acquaintances passed their days. Marcia was a nurse, although I never did discover if she was working. Her partner earned his living as a diver, catching crayfish, crab, and lobster when he could find them. He was part of a team of about half a dozen. Some had been up north, diving below the oil rigs being installed around Aberdeen and the Shetlands, doing maintenance work. It was well paid but dangerous. However, the divers there had access to good medical care and the availability of a decompression chamber, to prevent decompression sickness, known colloquially as "the bends". Self-employed divers were much more careless and, anxious to get to the surface, particularly if their catch had been meagre, often cut short their decompression time. Throughout that bizarre weekend I heard constant references to their intemperate haste to get to dry land and saw more than one rubbing an elbow or shoulder with a grimace of pain, where nitrogen bubbles had settled in the joint.

The weather was freezing. I was chilly in bed and slept badly. I felt the beginnings of a cold coming on and I longed for Dee's warmth beside me. The men had been hoping to dive on Saturday morning, but the weather was stormy, so they grouped in a local pub, taking it in turns to go down to the harbour and returning to report on little improvement. Marcia, Di and I wandered around Penzance, which I thought a dreary town. It had the desolate look common to most seaside towns in the winter. I thought Marazion much prettier, with its tiny twisting lanes and brightly painted cottages. The view out to St Michael's Mount was delightful.

I was astonished at Marcia, who seemed oblivious to the arctic conditions and wasn't even wearing a coat. She told me she didn't possess one. In the afternoon the weather improved, the wind dropped and it was sunny. We all went down to the harbour to see the men off; they had decided it was worth a go. In their diving gear they looked exotic and glamorous. The rubber wet suits and the heavy gas bottles on their backs leant a stern masculinity to their appearance and made me think of warriors going into battle. I thought we should be giving them "favours". The fact that they were engaged in a dangerous occupation, even one that they did voluntarily, made them appear courageous, bold and exciting. Any other job, by comparison, would be unadventurous.

It was pure fantasy. They were young, foolhardy and irresponsible, taking little care of their health. But if they were exotic in the freezing British winter, how much more must they have appeared in the summer, when they surfed off Cornwall's sandy beaches or taught scuba diving in the Caribbean. There their golden bodies and bleached hair would be competing with the multi-coloured fish darting in and out of the equally multi-coloured coral. I hope they made the best of it: "golden lads... all must, like chimney sweepers, come to dust", and so on, as Shakespeare wrote in *Cymbeline*. I was always a real sucker, as Di told me, for seeing the romantic in everything.

Leaving the men to their sub-aqua activities, we went off to see if we could find a fish and chip shop. I realized that apart from a piece of toast that morning we'd had nothing to eat since finishing Dee's sandwiches more than twenty-four hours previously.

The chippy was closed. The sign read "Open again May 1st". Di sighed. "That says it all regarding seaside towns in the winter. Hastings is just the same. I swear you can't buy tampons in any chemist between September and May." She had done her nursing training there and knew it well.

Hunger drove us onwards. Eventually we found a pie shop open and bought hot Cornish pasties, which were delicious.

The divers got back about 5:30 p.m., tired and dispirited. Their catch had been meagre: a few crayfish and several smallish crabs. An arrangement had been made for all the party, about a dozen of us, to have dinner in an old pub in Penzance. I found myself seated next to the tow-haired man with the deep laughter lines down his cheek; the one who'd commented on the dancer's breasts. As he sat down he kissed my cheek. "Hello," he said. "You look nice; I hope you don't mind my grabbing this place."

Actually I was delighted. Throughout the entire meal he never took his left hand from my thigh. His approach was so blatant and his intentions so obvious that I was overcome by a feeling of helplessness. There seemed a terrible inevitability about it all, and I felt swept up in it. I didn't feel threatened or intimidated; I didn't have that excuse. He was certainly devoid of Philippe's charm and sweetness, but there was a persuasive determination in him that was ridiculously compelling.

Standing at the bar, on my second brandy, I found Di beside me. She said quietly, "You are being a real fool, you know."

I couldn't meet her eyes but I nodded. "Yes, I probably am."

She continued, "We're leaving at 10 a.m. tomorrow and I won't wait!"

The spiral staircase in the diver's whitewashed fisherman's cottage led up to a bedroom hung with fishing nets, shells and artfully arranged pieces of driftwood. It was a lovely room, a room for lovers. We were scarcely that – more like ships that pass in the night. I didn't gain anything from this episode, though he was skilful and considerate. I slept fitfully, full of cold, coughing and sneezing, until the small hours when at last I fell into a deep sleep. I woke around 9:45 a.m. and scrambled frantically into my clothes. My companion drove me around to Marcia and Felix's flat. We arrived at 10:10 and Di had gone.

There were no trains on Sunday that could get me home, so I spent another twenty-four miserable hours in Marazion. First thing on Monday I went to the bank to withdraw money for my train fare. Marcia and Felix asked me for a £50 loan and I was so wretched I lent it to them. It seemed an appropriate penance, as I felt I had treated Di very badly. During the long journey home I had time to reflect on my stupidity. I was consumed with shame and regret, and could barely face the thought not only of my stupidity but clearly of my cupidity. I never got the £50 back either.

PART 2

Catalogue of Errors: Poole 1970–71

CHAPTER 9

Interlude

I had been afraid that there would be some coolness between Di and me after the Penzance fiasco, but by nature she was magnanimous and she may have felt a little sorry that she had stuck so rigidly to her word. I apologized very sincerely for having been selfish and thoughtless. Although we were both invited, I had gone as Di's guest, so it was singularly inappropriate for me to have gone off to do my own thing. I didn't discuss or attempt to explain the sort of spiritual and emotional desert I felt I was lost in. It was coming up to a year since I had left my convent and I felt I could argue a very good case for nuns leaving their community needing some serious preparation and guidance. However, I felt I had passed a watershed and, having made some serious errors of judgment, could now reassess where I wanted to be and how exactly I wanted to live my life.

I had not seen my father since leaving Liverpool, although we had written to each other. I had been preoccupied with my mother's problems, but with her happily established in Hove, I felt there was no excuse not to see him. He was working as a chef in a college in Oxford, so I went up to visit him and spent a weekend there. Cravenly I didn't reproach him for his treatment of my mother. In fact, I barely mentioned her, and as a result had a lovely time. He was always good at skating over difficult situations and did not easily accept challenges to his behaviour. I wasn't sure it would achieve anything and might possibly antagonize him. Typically he wanted to avoid any "unpleasantness", so asked briefly about her and then passed on to other things.

On a few other occasions Di came with me when I went to see him and we spent time wandering around the city and through the colleges' lovely golden quads, drinking in the pubs that I remembered from my pre-convent days. The Turf Tavern, tucked away down a little twisted entrance, was a must and seemed much the same, but I was sorry to find that The Mitre, the elegant and rather exclusive watering hole, had become a Beefeater pub. The bar in The Randolph had been re-decorated, but the barman, although not the one I remembered, was just as surly as his predecessor. Some things hadn't changed, such as the tiny intimate White Horse in Broad Street, sandwiched between two branches of Blackwell's bookshop. Here, the landlord, nearly ten years before, had refused to serve me on the grounds of my age, seeing through my pretend sophistication. The place was as delightful as ever and this time I got a drink.

Spring drifted into summer and in the interests of becoming a thoroughly modern woman, and encouraged by Di, I began driving lessons. She was generous in allowing me to drive her car so that I could get in some practice. As usual I was completely over-confident and failed the first test spectacularly.

Enid Baker, my colleague at St Richard's, was living in her parents' holiday cottage in West Wittering, only a few miles outside Chichester, and that long, lovely summer she often invited anyone who was free to come over. We sat in the garden, soaking up the sun. One of the nursery auxiliaries, who always had a beautiful tan, swore by a mixture of olive oil and lemon juice, so we copied her potion with enthusiasm. Enid complained that we stank the place out with vinaigrette; later, back in the unit, Sister Baines agreed. But it worked and we all had lovely tans. On cooler days we sat in Enid's pretty sitting room, drinking coffee or wine. Sometimes we went to the beach and occasionally swam. Going back on duty, if we had a split shift, we would be rather sunburnt, with sand between our toes and our backs itchy with salt. These were halcyon days, for me at any rate. I was calm and contented. I had friends and enough money. My family were settled; my mother was well and seemed happy, and I saw my father and brother regularly. At the flat we too entertained. I learned to cook more adventurously, and occasionally Lorenzo and some of the others from The Old Cross came for supper.

Dee was happy in her pregnancy. As we were sharing a bed I used to tease her, saying, "That baby of yours kicked hell out of me all night." She would just smile.

The extension of our lease meant we were secure in the flat until December, but we could see that there were decisions to be made. Dee was talking of moving in with Lorenzo, and Di and I began to think of a need to change our own situation. Neither of us wanted to be too far away from Chichester or Brighton and rather liked the south coast. Di vetoed Hastings on principle, as she had trained there and thought it such a dead end place in the winter. I didn't like the idea of Penzance either. The memory of my folly was too fresh in my mind, and I preferred to forget about my one night stand with the diver. Of course, I might have got my £50 back...

Eventually we settled on Poole and applied for staff midwife posts at the maternity hospital. We were called for interview and both of us offered jobs.

We did three things at the beginning of September. We gave our landlord notice that we would be moving out at the beginning of October, we handed in our notice at St Richard's, and Di and I went on holiday to Ibiza! The flight, and ten days' half-board in San Antonio, cost each of us £30 (about £400 today).

Our flight was at 11 p.m. We were accompanied, riotously, to Gatwick by all the boys from The Old Cross and headed straight for the bar, where we spent an hour or so downing various lurid cocktails. By the time we went through the gate for boarding, we were very much in the holiday spirit.

Ibiza, before the serious invasion of the "beautiful people" and the party culture, was a charmingly simple place and we had a delightful holiday. The season, by mid-September, was virtually over, so the white sandy beaches were sparsely populated and the Mediterranean, which had yet to become so disastrously polluted, was not only warm, but limpid. Beyond the coastal strip, higher up into the interior of the island, the countryside was beautiful, with tiny villages tucked away in the folds of the hills, which were covered with lush vegetation. Individual villas looked like white handkerchiefs sticking out of the breast pockets of loden green jackets.

Our simple hotel was clean and quiet; the one disadvantage was the sharing of a dining table with two honeymoon couples. Their conversation consisted almost entirely of a competitive comparison of the quality of their newly acquired crockery, and lamentations about the deficiency of the catering at their respective weddings. Eventually we got fed up with it. We might have coped had they not, once they had exhausted the relative virtues of oven to tableware against bone china, begun to complain vociferously about the hotel food. Given the cost of the holiday, we thought it was pretty good. In the end we took to eating either very early or as late as we could, so we had the table to ourselves.

We avoided the hotel pool, which was often crowded. Instead, we took a little rickety bus to a different beach every day. The beach cafés were cheap and as far as we could tell clean; in any event we suffered no ill effects until the very last day when unwisely I ate squid. I developed a real taste for Bacardi and coke and was amazed at the quantity poured into the glass; there were no optic measures here. We drank, sunbathed and swam, read and snoozed, and in the evening found little bars where handsome Spaniards played acoustic guitars and flirted with pretty girls. Dockets for drinks were clipped together with a clothes peg and settled by paying an ancient crone at the door as you left. Everybody seemed very honest. There was nothing to prevent surreptitious removal of one or several dockets, but I never saw it happen.

One evening, we went to the typical tourist show: Spanish dancers with lots of ruffles and castanets; not real flamenco but good fun none the less. We avoided the other "events", deciding that learning to drink from a bota was not essential for either our professional or our social life. Instead we hired a car and drove across the island to Santa Eulalia, quieter and more elegant than San Antonio but with equally beautiful beaches and a palm tree lined promenade.

It was an idyllic holiday, but I was not able to put out of my mind the memory of some of the recent events for which I felt great regret and which persisted in intruding. There were times I found it hard, those warm sunlit days, lying in the shade with so little noise except the hissing to and fro of the waves in my ears, not to reflect, with some agitation, on the past eighteen months. Questions troubled me and floated to the surface of my mind like scum on stagnant water. How was it possible to have changed so much? How and why had I drifted so rapidly away from self-control and taken on a way of life so diametrically opposed to what had gone before? Was I really so shallow; a pleasure seeker; a hedonist? Above all, how had I moved away from the practice of my faith? This bothered me most. I still believed it all and found I missed the sacraments. So, occasionally, in a fit of remorse, I went to Mass and communion, but in truth felt I was fleeing the church. I was uncertain why, but it caused me some torment.

Ten days passed too quickly; the holiday was over. I was going back to start a new chapter in a new town, a new hospital, new accommodation. Poole, I felt sure, was going to be a happy place. I was going to give up the madness of the last few months and become a well-balanced woman, ready, as they say, to fulfil all my potential. Whatever could go wrong?

CHAPTER 10

Roses Round the Door

Poole was generally considered an excellent place to live. It was certainly affluent, a desirable location. The big money had not yet arrived, but the size of the properties, the proximity of the sea, the beautiful beaches, and the general belief that, like Bournemouth, it benefited from a microclimate, were all beginning to generate the interest that would rapidly engulf it. In 1970 it was quiet, comfortable and safe. It encouraged me to believe that we had made a good choice. The staff-midwife's post at the maternity unit was a hospital appointment. I was not an agency nurse any more. I would have paid holidays and, if I was off sick, my salary was assured.

We found accommodation easily in Lilliput, a charming suburb, close to the sea. It was a pleasant single-storey dwelling with, even in September, late flowering roses round the door and a few hollyhocks up the path. There were two bedrooms, a tiny living room with kitchen off it, and a bathroom. It looked ideal. We noticed the lack of central heating, but we hadn't had that in Chichester either, and looking around at the small size of our new accommodation we thought that some sort of radiant heating might do the job if we were cold. I hoped that our social life would be so wonderful that we would only use the place for sleeping in.

"Poole!" people said. "How wonderful. The sailing fraternity will certainly welcome you. They always need people to crew for them." I wasn't quite sure what "crewing" meant, but it sounded fun and I was prepared to give it a go. Would we have to join a sailing club? Was it very expensive? We moved in about a week before starting at the hospital.

From the first day at the unit I felt uneasy. Not the usual uneasiness or sense of dislocation that normally occurs when you have to adapt to a new situation, a change of job or position, but something closer to serious apprehension. The senior midwives in charge of the wards seemed to have been there for ever; to be part of the fabric of the building. With one or two exceptions, there was a noticeable lack of warmth. I didn't feel there was any of the camaraderie I had been so used to in Chichester or Liverpool.

Di and I were working in separate departments, she in the antenatal ward and I in postnatal, so we had little or no contact during the day. After the intimacy of St Richard's, the place seemed unwelcoming and bleak. There was a sort of dreariness, a "brownness", about the whole place. It didn't help that the uniform of the senior staff was beige.

This was enhanced by one particularly and personally unattractive feature. The matron was a serious smoker. I didn't object to that as everybody seemed to puff away then, but her particular manner of smoking involved deep exhalation through her nose, so that her nostrils and upper lip were stained with nicotine and her breath was heavy with tobacco smoke. There was something reptilian about her. All interaction with her was a trial of endurance. I found her physically repulsive and socially repellent. There is only so long one can hold one's breath to avoid being overwhelmed by halitosis. The other senior midwives were competent but distant and chilly, and not very interested in admitting other qualified staff to their ranks. There was always a slight stiffness and lack of warmth, a feeling of "them and us".

I tried to overcome my antipathy, both to the staff and to the setup, telling myself that I'd get used to it; that one needs time to adapt; that every job is different, and there are some things that one enjoys more than others in any working environment. I suspected that Di felt the same, although initially neither of us said anything.

After a couple of weeks, I came home to find her slouched in the sitting room. She looked up and said unequivocally, "I don't know what you think, but I think we've made a mistake. It's grim."

I could only agree, but the statement threw me into a state of acute anxiety. If Di, who was normally so upbeat and positive about things, had qualms, then we were in trouble.

"What are we going to do?" I asked.

"There's nothing much we can do about it yet," she replied. "We've got to stay six months, haven't we?" Six months was the minimum time before you could reasonably leave a job after being appointed. The winter months stretched ahead.

Even our accommodation was proving to be far less satisfactory than we had hoped. The roses round the door inevitably faded as October progressed, and the hollyhocks died back. Our little bungalow, so charming in September, was uncomfortably chilly in October, from a total lack of insulation. Even from the outside it looked bleak. It was jerry built and one brick thick, so it was clear that we would need more than an electric fire to heat the place. In the end we bought a paraffin heater, which was reasonably efficient in keeping the bungalow warm, but was to generate other problems later.

A more significant lack was the absence of a decent pub close by. Lilliput was a residential area and our road had neither shop nor hostelry. Without a car we would have been very isolated indeed. We took to buying wine and spirits from the off-licence and tried to restrict ourselves during the week to one glass in the evening. If I was on my own, it was a real temptation not to ward off the chill with a brandy and ginger, or even two! I missed the buzz and liveliness of the atmosphere in The Old Cross.

For a brief moment, something that did liven things up a little, if only for its oddity, was the discovery of an aunt who lived in the area. I had completely forgotten about her until my mother reminded me. She was not a blood relation, being the wife of my mother's eldest brother, but a maternal aunt-in-law. I had vague memories of having met her when I was a child, and had heard her mentioned in the family circle later on. Her name was Rita, and she had married when she was only sixteen, because, as my mother told me ominously, "she had to". Rita never received a very good press from my mother. I don't think it was the pregnancy, the out-of-wedlock stigma, but rather that the young couple (her husband

Archie was also only sixteen) had moved into my grandparents' Glaswegian home, a terraced house in the then rural suburb of Govan. The place was very crowded. My mother, who at eight was the baby of the family, lost her bedroom and had to sleep in a cupboard bed in the kitchen. This did not endear Rita to her.

"She was very keen to have a piano," my mother told me. "We had absolutely no space for one."

"Did she play?"

"Not at all. She just thought having a piano would bring her up in the world."

Privately, I thought Aunt Rita must have been quite a feisty lady and I didn't think there was anything wrong in trying to move up in the world. Social mobility it's called today, and most people are for it. In any event Aunt Rita and Uncle Archie moved very steadily upwards. His hard work took him from office boy to director of several companies, including a company then known as British Thermotank, so Rita had every reason to be proud.

Di and I went out to Parkstone, where she and Archie were living. The house was large, beautiful and expensively furnished. The carpets were cream, and the minute she opened the door, she asked us to take off our shoes. I am always astonished at this, although I know it is customary in many countries. Why, I wonder, put carpets down, particularly cream or white ones, if you are afraid people will walk on them? It wasn't as if we had come from the farmyard, with wellies covered in manure. However, we did as she requested.

She offered us a drink and poured generous gin and tonics. She asked politely after my mother and the family, and I asked after hers. She said how sorry she was that my parents had broken up. All very civilized. Then she suddenly demanded, "Has Colin still got his wonderful head of hair?" My father did have a lovely head of hair, thick, black and glossy. She was looking beyond me, as if at some pleasant memory, and smiling a little, and it occurred to me that she must have been very pretty as a young woman. "He had such fine dark eyes," she added, and smiled again. I would have been willing to bet that my father had stolen the odd kiss or two; her little secret smile suggested a romantic memory.

She said that her husband, Archie, was out that evening. "He's away out to spend the evening with Young Archie." One of the peculiarities of my mother's side of the family was the persistence of the name Archie. My maternal grandfather was Archie, as was his eldest son, my uncle Archie. His son, my cousin, was known as "Young Archie" and his son was called "Wee Archie". I thought it led to confusion, but apparently it's a Scottish thing. There was uproar when my parents named my brother Peter. "There's never been a Peter in the family!" was my grandmother's complaint. In time my own brother called his son Joshua Archie, ironically I hoped.

My uncle was, Rita told me, becoming so very forgetful that she couldn't let him go out by himself. "Young Archie had to come and pick him up," she observed peevishly. That seemed to irritate her. "He forgets everything; I don't think he makes any effort. Do you know why I think that?"

I didn't answer; she was obviously going to tell me.

"Because he can still play bridge! He can remember every card that's been played. Now why can he play bridge but can't find his way to the garage?"

I was at a loss as to know what to say, so I just smiled sympathetically. Conversation with Rita was rather like hitting a ball against a wall. It always came back faster than expected and often from oblique angles; very much a one-sided event. As we were leaving, I commented on a particularly beautiful vase of Venetian glass. The iridescent colours glowed in the gentle lighting of her room. "That's gorgeous, Aunt Rita!"

"Och, no," she replied, her mouth turned down disparagingly, and added, "It's all rubbish abroad." In that pithy phrase, she condemned the entirety of European art treasures, culture and good taste. We laughed in amazement all the way home.

I didn't see much of Rita, or Archie for that matter, although I visited him a couple of times when he was in hospital for some unspecified complaint. His dementia was very evident. Rita sat restlessly beside him, getting up now and again to rearrange the cards on his locker or to refold clean clothes that she had brought in for him.

"This isn't my house, is it?" he asked, looking around anxiously. He repeated the question several times, adding on one sad occasion, "Are you my wife? Are you Rita?"

At last she snapped. "You know full well who I am, Archie! Of course it isn't your house; the walls in our house have lovely wallpaper."

I thought this response was as unhelpful as it was sharp, but when I glanced at her, I saw her eyes were full of tears. Pity welled up in me.

It was my first encounter with dementia (although it would not be my last) and it filled me with dismay and a sort of gothic horror. Into what dark, alien and lonely land had my poor uncle wandered? How frightened he must feel, lost in the tangled undergrowth of his mind.

CHAPTER 11

Mould, Mildew and Other Issues

November was bleak. The wind blew salty air inland, so even had we been able to hang our washing out, it would never have dried. The nearest launderette was in Broadstone, not really within walking distance, so the bathroom was constantly festooned with dripping smalls. These undoubtedly contributed to the all-pervading atmosphere of humidity.

Our paraffin heater, which was efficient in generating warmth, was also generating water vapour. The walls were permanently damp with condensation, and in the morning when I put my hand on the bedcovers it felt as if they were covered with dew.

"We are going to get home one day and find this place has melted. There will be nothing except a pile of wet rubble," I told Di.

Our first weekend off together we headed straight back to Chichester and the elegant comfort and warm welcome of Di's parents' flat. Maxine was horrified when we described our accommodation. "It will ruin your health; you will have permanent chest infections. You are going to have to move!" To comfort me she introduced me to the pleasures of a "mixed Martini", half dry, half sweet vermouth; I found it delicious. Sustained with several glasses, we spent an entire evening discussing our accommodation.

We had contemplated moving and talked about it, but the sheer hassle of giving notice to the landlord, finding somewhere else, moving out and moving in did not seem to be worth the effort, particularly as we had more or less decided that we would only stay in Poole for six months. We felt we could grin and bear it.

Maxine's view of the health issue was not without substance and we suffered from frequent coughs and colds. I began to feel generally rather unwell, an unspecific malaise of aches and pains, and the occasional temperature, with a slight but persistent ache low down in my abdomen that became acute when I was menstruating. I wondered if I had a fibroid.

None of this helped me to come to terms with our living arrangements and was exacerbated by my dissatisfaction with my work environment. This remained as unfriendly as ever. It is difficult to pinpoint why some hospitals are more pleasant than others. It isn't to do with the building, for nothing could have been less prepossessing than the exterior of the maternity unit at St Richard's and yet inside all was cheeriness and light. Poole Maternity was a medium-sized hospital, relatively busy, but neither as large nor as busy as Liverpool Maternity Hospital where I had trained as a midwife. There had been no lack of warmth there. I think the layout, with the antenatal and postnatal wards on different floors, was a factor, because of the lack of integration of the services. Poole was not a training school either, so we had no student midwives, who are always guaranteed to liven a place up a bit.

Above all I missed antenatal care and delivering babies. Even when a new midwife arrived, the overall mood didn't lighten. She was a cheerful girl whose breezy temperament seemed defined by her buttercup yellow Morris 1000 and her vivid red lipstick. She was asked to tone the lipstick down after a week or so – a directive that I am happy to say she ignored. "This place isn't very jolly, is it?" she said one lunchtime – a rhetorical question that clearly needed no response. She came from Poole and had a boyfriend in Bournemouth, so she put up with the disadvantages, as she had home comforts and a social life to cheer her up. Unlike me she seemed to take it all in her stride.

One of the consequences of job dissatisfaction, I discovered, was that my mind was not sufficiently concentrated on my job.

I began to make mistakes: not life-threatening mistakes but careless and unnecessary ones. My paperwork became unreliable, which obviously reinforced the poor opinion that senior staff had of me. On one awful occasion, I forgot to notify parents in the waiting room that the ambulance to transport their sick baby to Southampton had arrived. Consequently it left without them. Even worse, not only had I failed to notify them, but I had completely forgotten the entire incident. So when the next morning the senior sister approached me, her eyes as cold as a fish, and said, "You surpassed yourself yesterday evening," I couldn't think what she was talking about.

I was speechless with horror when I realized my mistake. My letter of apology to the parents was taken in good part. They were charmingly forgiving and the baby was fine, but I was never closer to giving up midwifery all together. I was lucky to escape without an official reprimand.

When we had first started work in Poole, we asked that our booked holidays be honoured, as is normal, and it was rather grudgingly agreed. So with a certain amount of cheek, we said we had holidays booked over Christmas. This did not endear us to our seniors, although I heard one of them saying she "preferred to spend the festive season on the ward because it was always so jolly". Certainly if one had no family, the hospital environment had a certain appeal. My mother was spending Christmas with Linda's parents in Brighton and although I was also invited, I declined on the grounds of a previous invitation from Di's mother.

Packing for the visit, Di made an unpleasant discovery.

"Look at this." She held out a pretty woollen skirt mottled with black stains, for my inspection. "What is it?" She pulled several other things from her wardrobe, only to find the same black flecks on all of them. We peered dubiously at the clothes.

"Di, I think it's mildew. You know, mould." The cupboard smelled damp.

"Will it come off?" She looked close to tears.

"I'm not sure, but I don't think so. It's in the very fabric of the cloth."

The discovery both appalled and depressed us. My clothes had largely escaped, but many of Di's were ruined. The quality of hers was much better than mine, for she was able to acquire garments at cost price from her mother's elegant boutique. Our social life had been so non-existent, we'd had few opportunities to go anywhere other than the hospital. In the morning, we put on our uniforms and in the evening, when we got home, we put on our night things and wrapped ourselves in blankets. We'd had little occasion to wear anything else and so our things had hung undisturbed in the cupboard. The mould just seemed to sum up all we felt about our life in Poole.

As we drove back to Chichester across the moorland area of the New Forest around Ringwood, everything became lighter. As I looked out at the bronzed, bracken-covered land and saw groups of the tough little ponies grazing there, I felt as if I were surfacing from a trough of despond. I was even able to joke about it all.

"We've got ten whole days away from the place. Do you think they'd miss us if we never went back? It's not as if we ever really integrated."

The idea of never going back was so appealing that we began to laugh, but our laughter had a certain edge of hysteria to it.

Christmas was delightful. Dee came over to the flat in the evenings, blooming in her pregnancy. Maxine was in her element, fussing over us and giving advice, whether it was asked for or not, in her usual forthright manner. We reclaimed The Old Cross with enthusiasm. And Poole faded a little. But my abdominal pain seemed worse over the next few days and eventually I got an appointment with the GP I'd been registered with in Chichester.

He sat back in his chair after examining me and looked at me over the steeple of his fingers. "You've got a fibroid, I think. You really ought to come into hospital for tests – you'll probably need to have it out. Sooner rather than later. It's not a serious operation but there is also some tenderness there. You get a temperature now and again, do you?" He paused. "You might have a pelvic inflammatory condition too."

He was too much of a gentleman to ask me what I'd been getting up to, but the unspoken question hung in the air. I could almost see the bubble above his head, with the words in capital letters and red ink: STD.

"I'll refer you to a gynaecologist in Poole," he said, handing me a letter. Cheekily, after leaving his consulting room, I opened it and was startled to find myself described as "This rather odd girl…".

"Am I odd?" I asked Di.

"Not *odd*, exactly, but not really run of the mill either."

In some ways I thought it was a kind of compliment.

The drive back to Poole was miserable. We travelled in depressed silence. The cottage after the Christmas break was even less welcoming, but surprisingly the atmosphere in the maternity unit seemed less gloomily repressive. I was moved to the special baby care unit, where the senior sister was at least affable. None of the infants were particularly unwell, as Southampton took the really poorly ones, so in some respects it was similar to St Richard's. The babies were kept warm and fed, and given oxygen if they had respiratory problems and light therapy if they were jaundiced. Once or twice I saw an exchange transfusion for babies suffering from rhesus incompatibility. We put a teaspoonful of brandy into their milk to sedate them and they usually just went off to sleep. I often wondered about the effects of such an amount of alcohol on the livers of these small creatures. A teaspoon of brandy in less than 100 mls of milk is not a weak dilution and it did occur to me that it might give them quite a significant hangover.

Thanks to my GP's referral, I got an appointment to see the gynaecologist at Poole General very quickly. He was very pleasant and very thorough and spoke of operating within the month. He agreed about the fibroid, which he said was about the size of an apple; a thought that made me feel as if I had a fruit tree growing inside me. He made no bones about the pelvic inflammatory condition. "It's probably chlamydia," he grinned sympathetically. "I see a lot of it, I'm afraid, but it could be worse. We'll soon have you sorted. Let's have a look at you."

As with any examination of that kind, there was a certain amount of prodding and poking, and the next morning I woke in considerable discomfort and with a temperature of 39 degrees. I took several days' sick leave.

The weather was arctic, with blustery gusts and even sleet; so much for Poole's microclimate. I lay shivering in bed surrounded by hot water bottles and wondering how much longer this misery would last. After a few days, with my temperature down to normal, I staggered shakily back to work but felt wretched.

Di took a rushed trip home to Chichester to get her car its MOT, only to have it fail on her! Lorenzo, kind and supportive as ever, lent her his, which got her back to Poole. We seemed to be just staggering from one crisis to another.

"Things really can't get any worse," I told Di, with what transpired to be very misplaced optimism.

On 20 January the postal workers went on strike. Postboxes were sealed, and in those pre-mobile phone days, communication ground to a halt. We might just as well have been in the Outer Hebrides.

CHAPTER 12

Lost in Lilliput

During the periods of sick leave, lying in bed, I had a great deal of time to think about things and to reflect on how I had spent the past eighteen or so months. I remembered a patient I had nursed in Broadgreen who had been convinced that her health problems were a visitation from God, a punishment for past offences. I had pitied her, as her distress was heartfelt, but had thought her deluded. Now I wasn't so sure. Not that I blamed God – I didn't blame anyone except myself – but my problems were undoubtedly the consequences of my own actions. I felt full of self-pity and must have been a real drag to live with.

"Look," said Di briskly, "it's an infection. Anyone, if they are sexually active, married or not, can get it, but you can make a moral case out of it if you want, if it makes you feel better. You Catholics and your guilt!"

She was quite right; I was prepared to flagellate myself over it, mentally. In an effort to try and get everything in proportion, I set off one afternoon to the nearest Catholic church and sought out the parish priest. He was very cool, positively unfriendly, and I think irritated about being disturbed in the afternoon without an appointment.

"You should have rung," he said petulantly. "People usually ring."

"I'm sorry, Father; I don't have easy access to a phone."

"We'd better go into the church. My housekeeper isn't in, and I don't interview young women in the presbytery on their own."

I didn't know if the implication was that I would assault him or that he, finding me irresistible, might throw himself on me.

I was beginning to feel like a scarlet woman and regretted coming. I followed him sheepishly into the church and sat down uneasily beside him. He smelled of stale tobacco and a pungent aftershave, Old Spice perhaps. Once he heard that I had been a nun, he became embarrassed and wouldn't look at me. I got a lot of mumbling about there being more joy in heaven over one repentant sinner than over all the just. He cleared his throat a lot. Then to my horror he began to talk about God being ready to forgive me, as he had probably punished me enough. I looked at him in disbelief.

"I don't think God is punishing me," I protested. "I never thought God was punishing me."

"You deserve to be punished," he replied sharply. "Your life since you left your convent, from what you tell me, has been one of self-indulgence and sin. This is no way for an ex-nun to behave." He waited in silence, then said abruptly, "Would you like to make your confession now?"

I studied his pale round face and sandy hair and the network of thread veins on his nose and chin. I didn't think this was the right way to go about bringing me back into the bosom of the church. I sat in silence for a moment or two looking at the sanctuary lamp winking at the side of the altar, at the statue of Our Lady of Lourdes, and beyond her the ubiquitous form of Saint Thérèse of Lisieux, with her armful of roses. Despite her mawkish image, I have always felt her to be one of the truly heroic saints.

It was all so sweetly familiar; the lump in my throat was so huge I couldn't speak. I heard the priest sigh impatiently, so I just smiled at him, got up, genuflected toward the tabernacle and left him sitting there. The holy water stoop needed refilling, but there was enough to dip my finger and cross myself. The door shut quietly behind me. I whispered to myself, "I will come back."

I walked for some distance to try and calm myself and to put the unpleasant and unhelpful interview behind me, and eventually caught a bus down to the marina. The waterfront was almost deserted and there was a bitter little wind blowing. Hugging my coat round me, I walked along the pontoon between the moorings, my shoes echoing loudly on the wooden boardwalk. I sat down on a stone bollard and lit a cigarette.

The smoke hung in the chilly air like a miasma. The boats bobbed sullenly in the water as if they were unhappy to be there, occasionally nudging each other sluggishly. I heard the slap and suck of the tide against their hulls, and the ping, ping, ping of halyards, tapping against the metal masts. The sea was oily and pewter grey. The occasional herring gull wheeled and pitched above me. Ahead, two juveniles, mottled brown, their beaks not yet yellow with the distinctive red spot, squabbled and tugged over some unidentifiable jetsam, screeching and pecking at each other. I felt ill with desolation and suspended in misery. Above the horizon, great rolling clouds gathered and loomed. Heading landwards, they looked full of snow. It was a bleak outlook. "Clouds like the wrath of God" – a favourite description of Sister Margaret from my Mary-Mount days – came to mind. The wrath of God? Surely not; not the God I knew, anyway.

On the way back to Lilliput I thought about what a disappointment Poole had been, but in fairness perhaps the fault was ours. Expectations had certainly been high: lots of sailing and lovely tanned men around. We had planned our move badly; winter is not the time of year for sailing, except for the fanatical. The main difficulty for us was linking up with sailors looking for crew. We couldn't just turn up at a boat club hoping to be welcomed in as new blood. I would certainly not have been audacious enough to breeze into one and expect to find an enthusiastic "yachty" willing to take me on. You might be lucky, meet someone casually who needs manpower on their boat, or be introduced at a party or in a pub. But if you join a sailing club, there is a hefty subscription, or a membership fee. Anyway, during our time in that elegant and affluent town, we almost never went out. Certainly the golden boys of our dreams were conspicuous by their absence. "They are all away sailing in the Caribbean, and we are lost in Lilliput," I told Di.

And the postal strike isolated us even more. We used the public phone in the hospital to contact our families, and the ward sisters said that in case of any emergency our families could contact us via the hospital switchboard.

A particular irritation was the delay in receiving a form from my father relating to the purchase of a sewing machine. Before Christmas I had gone into Bournemouth to buy one. I chose a nifty little Singer and was offered the possibility of buying it on credit. As it was rather more expensive than I had hoped, I elected to pay over six months. The agreement was duly filled in and then to my astonishment I was told it would need to be countersigned or ratified by a man in the family, one in employment.

"Do you have a father or a brother nearby, who could sign it for you?"

"My father lives in Oxford; my brother in Portsmouth. I earn more than either of them. This is ridiculous!"

They tried to be helpful, saying they would reserve the machine for me. I was not placated, but there was no way round it; I had to get my father's or Peter's signature, or no sewing machine. In those days, single women, no matter how old or how well paid, could not get a mortgage on their own, so I suppose it was not surprising that I couldn't buy a sewing machine on credit.

So, the dispatched form was somewhere between Oxford and Poole or Poole and Oxford, lost in the recesses of some sorting office. Although the postal strike was not a specifically Poole thing, it added to our discontent. The strike lasted seven awful weeks and even when it was over, it took almost as long to sort out the backlog. In the end I bought a machine in Chichester and Di's father, pretending to be my own father, signed the form for me.

Chapter 13

Aftermath

I had my operation mid-February. It was all straightforward, no complications, so I made an uneventful recovery. My surgeon was honest and direct, if rather apologetic.

"It was a bit of a mess in there, I'm afraid. The fibroid was big, a big apple, but you'll be glad to know we didn't find a tree." He grinned. "The fibroid would have given you problems later, but the real issue was what to do with the ovary, which was polycystic. The fallopian tube was very scarred and, as tubes go, virtually useless. So we took those out." He paused. "I must tell you that although the other ovary looks fine, it is very likely that the remaining tube will have been affected. We have irrigated it with hydrocortisone and we'll just keep our fingers crossed. This sort of situation with a fallopian tube damaged by an infection can lead to fertility problems. You need to be aware of that."

So after a week (people stayed in hospital much longer in those days) I went back to the bungalow minus a fibroid and with only one ovary and its attendant fallopian tube. The continued inconvenience of the postal strike made it difficult for me to tell my mother. She had no phone in her flat but I was able to reach her at her office and eventually contacted my father, who in turn contacted my brother. It was all very time-consuming and frequently frustrating. I avoided giving the family details of my state of health and just said I'd had a fibroid removed. My mother was all set to come down to Poole to see me, but I put her off. I couldn't put her up, and I don't think she would have wanted to stay with Rita, the only other option.

Once I had recovered from the effects of the surgery I began to

Our wedding day, 10 November 1973. Even the rain didn't spoil the day.

A sunny "Roman holiday", autumn 1974.

Left: Honeymoon in Australia, the "Three Sisters" of New South Wales in the background, March 1974.

Left: The doting mother and little Esme, November 1976.

Below: Back from court after Esme's interim adoption order, December 1976. What a Christmas present!

Esme aged two. She always refused to pose!

Above: "Shush, Mummy, we are bringing you a bottle of wine!" 1979

"No, he can't play with my doll's house." 1979

Below: It took time for Esme and Paul to get used to each other! Summer 1979

Above: The hopper was actually Paul's.

Paul, my little schoolboy canary, on his first day at Glenhurst pre-school. September 1981

Friends! Paul, aged six, with Esme, aged eight, wearing her favourite grey velvet dress and posing as ever with great reluctance.

Paul and Esme enjoying ice creams on holiday in wonderful Walberswick, summer 1981.

Paul aged around seven or eight. This horror of a frog was his choice. It accompanied him everywhere he went.

Paul aged around ten. What's going on in his head? Mischief? Summer 1983

Right: Paul, aged four. How he loved this shabby old tricycle.

Below: Older, and a bigger, better bike. 1989

Esme, my lovely girl, aged fourteen
(left) and sixteen (below).

A family gathering to celebrate Mum and Dad's ruby wedding in 1981.
From left to right:
Back row: James (Ed and Annie's eldest son), Ed (brother of John), John, Eric (Lizzie's husband)
Middle row: Lizzie (sister of John and Ed), Mum, Dad (my lovely parents-in-law), Annie (Ed's wife), Oliver (youngest son of Annie and Ed), me!
Front row: Esme, Paul, and Eric and Lizzie's little boy, William.

feel considerably better. I could do as much or as little as I pleased. Di nagged me into taking some gentle exercise, and within a month I was back at work.

We had made up our minds about leaving Poole and began to scour the pages of the nursing magazines for jobs. In those days you could pretty well get a job anywhere. It was just a matter of applying. We decided against returning to St Richard's, as it seemed such an admission of failure, so when Di suggested St Mary's Maternity Hospital in Portsmouth on the strength of having trained for her midwifery diploma there, I was easily persuaded.

The postal strike had ended in early March but the backlog dragged on, so on our next day off together we drove to Portsmouth and applied there and then, leaving Di's mother's phone number as a contact. We were summoned for interview, fortunately on the same day, and both offered a sisters post. I had had my self-confidence so shaken by my time at Poole that I had applied for a staff midwife's job, but the matron at St Mary's expressed surprise, saying, "No, no. I've got two spaces to fill and you have been qualified long enough now! You are perfectly eligible for a sister's post." I wasn't going to refuse; I was delighted. However, the senior midwife in Poole said dismissively, "We are surprised. Staff Midwife Mann is clearly up to taking a sister's post, but I think you, Staff Midwife Stewart, have some way to go."

"Old bitch," said Di, deliberately loudly, when we left the office. I didn't hold it against her. My career at Poole had been far from glorious. So we handed in our notice, and after barely six unhappy months shook the dust of Poole from our feet and headed back to what we hoped would be sunnier climes in Hampshire.

We were delirious with relief and the journey back to Chichester was unmitigated pleasure, despite the discomfort. The car was stuffed to the gunwales, the ironing board and broom sticking out of the rear windows; pots, pans, crockery and cutlery clattering about in the boot; books, records, clothes and bedding tucked around us. I hoped we wouldn't need to stop, as I was completely penned in.

The New Forest had never looked so beautiful, the new bracken a tender green, the spring heather showing misty pink beneath the brazen yellow of the gorse, its lovely coconut smell wafting in through the open window behind me. It made the draught blowing down the back of my neck bearable.

Once again we were in Chichester, in Maxine's flat. We had a week before starting at St Mary's in Portsmouth and fecklessly treated that time as a holiday. We should have been finding somewhere to live, but we had been offered hospital accommodation and decided that we would take that temporarily and look around carefully. I was determined not to be fooled again by a few hollyhocks, or roses round the door.

We went to see Dee and Lorenzo and to admire Louise, their beautiful new dark-haired baby girl. Holding that warm, sweet-smelling little body in my arms, I was overcome with such yearning I could hardly speak. Dee saw my face and put her arms around me.

"You'll have your own one day."

Thinking of recent events, I was by no means certain. Although I struggled to put that dark thought to the back of my mind, it was ever-present, and it only needed a comment about motherhood to have me anxiously remembering the details of what the surgeon in Poole had told me. I tried to respond light-heartedly and laughed, "I'll need to find someone as nice as Lorenzo, and that's not going to be easy."

Dee smiled and Lorenzo looked bashful and blushed, and so the moment passed. They both seemed very happy and were making plans for their future, which involved, among other things, opening a restaurant. We thought they were very brave and admired their drive and ambition.

Poole was behind us, Portsmouth ahead. The evening before we were due to start our new jobs we went to The Old Cross.

"Just don't talk to me ever again about sailing and all those available men," I told Di over a large glass of wine.

"Portsmouth's a naval port, which means ships and sailors. What can I say?" She laughed and went to get another drink.

PART 3

A New Beginning: Portsmouth 1971-76

CHAPTER 14

A Sister Once Again

St Mary's Hospital started life in the mid-nineteenth century as a workhouse, but moved steadily upmarket, first to an infirmary in the late twenties, and finally acquiring the status of a hospital in the early thirties. It was a typical red-brick Victorian institution, but did have some claims to elegance. Thomas Owen, a well-respected architect, had been responsible for the design of the original central block, which was not without classical reference. Sadly, for its architectural integrity, the rest of the hospital began to spread both in height and length until it covered many acres. The paediatric department was actually on the other side of the main road. It was a mishmash of traditional hospital design and a collection of haphazard additions. The main three-storey building was divided by a long central corridor, with wards radiating from it. This thoroughfare was about a quarter of a mile long, and as busy as a motorway. Trolleys and wheelchairs jostled for passing space with the walking wounded, and nurses, medical staff and visitors wove determinedly between them. The signs designating the various wards or departments were often unclear, confusing or both, and the outpatients department issued maps to anyone needing to venture further afield. The whole place had more than a passing resemblance to Broadgreen Hospital in Liverpool. I loved it.

We were given accommodation right at the end of the main corridor, conveniently close to the canteen and even more conveniently close to the League of Friends' shop, where we could buy biscuits and instant coffee, as well as chocolates, ham and cheese rolls, and soft drinks. We were very snug, with our own bathroom; we even had a television in our rooms. Above all, we had no interference from the possible tyranny of a "home sister" whose job was to issue late passes and supervise the student nurses. I never did discover the purpose of this little oasis. Possibly it had been used by housemen on call or perhaps for the permanent night sisters, but it was quiet and warm. My window looked out onto a yard filled with huge wheelie bins bulging with dirty linen destined for the laundry. Not the most pleasant of views, but I reasoned that my stay in hospital accommodation would be relatively short, so was prepared to overlook it.

The maternity unit, a later addition in the sixties, was attached to the main hospital by a short spur. A four-storey rectangular building, it was uncompromisingly modern. Below and between each window was a coloured panel, so the whole thing looked rather like a Rubik's Cube. But it was purpose built and looked smart and reassuring. Everything about it delighted me. It certainly didn't feel "brown". The receptionists that first morning smiled and directed me to the matron's office. Miss Upman suited the nomenclature "matron" perfectly. She was indeed matronly; her full rounded bosom looked as if it could be the perfect cushion for any distressed head to lean into. She had neat feet, beautifully shod in pristine black lace-ups; her frilled cap was immaculately white and stiff like a meringue. It perched like a crown on top of her head. I was greeted with friendly briskness and taken by her up to the first floor, A2, my allocated ward.

I was surprised about how anxious I was. Poole had unnerved me and I felt a real new girl. The ward was busy, but the welcome was warm and similar to the one I'd had at St Richard's.

"We are really pleased to have you!" said Anthea Seal, the senior midwife, a tall, handsome woman. "We are always looking for more staff." I found I had joined a team of four full-time midwifery sisters, a few part-time staff midwives and a handful of auxiliary nurses, so I didn't feel they were short at all, certainly compared to Poole. But the catchment area for Portsmouth, I discovered, was huge and the city was one of the most densely populated in the UK. The unit was always busy.

What particularly delighted me was the integration, on all the wards, of antenatal and postnatal care. Ward A3 on the other side of the building was a mirror image of A2, and the four labour rooms, in a central block, were shared between us. This pattern was repeated on the second and third floors. The layout meant in effect that the patients had a certain continuity of care, because they weren't moved to a different ward after the birth of the baby. They saw the same familiar faces. On the top floor were the theatre suite and the high-tech baby care unit, with its own specialized staff.

Di, on the floor above me, was very much in her element. Her student midwife days meant St Mary's was very familiar to her, so the adaptation was not hard, but I settled in very quickly too. Within a week I felt at home and the experience of Poole began to fade from my mind; in time I even joked about it. St Mary's worked a straight shift system, no more splits, which was a relief; night duty cropped up about every six weeks.

Another pleasant feature was the presence of pupil midwives on the wards. As a qualified midwife I had a serious and important teaching role, something I enjoyed very much. At twenty-eight I was several years older than most of them. I found it strange but not unpleasant to be deferred to politely, to be asked for advice and to hear my name, "Sister Stewart". I hadn't been Sister Stewart since leaving Liverpool. I tried to remember how overawed I had been with *my* first delivery and how dreadfully inadequate I had felt. I hope I was kind and gentle with the less self-assured pupils and firmly in control with the impetuous ones, of which there were plenty.

Trying to encourage and help a new mother with feeding her baby, I discovered that Portsmouth women had the same outgoing raunchiness that I had first come across in Liverpool.

"I just can't get my baby to fasten onto my nipple," a young woman told me, close to tears. The pupil midwife trying to help her was having no success either.

"Don't worry, love!" her adjacent bedfellow reassured her. "If he's a boy, he won't take long to get the hang of it!" There was raucous laughter all around. I tried to keep a straight face, but the pupil midwife snorted with embarrassed laugåhter.

Apart from the midwifery staff, the ancillary support was excellent too.

I was charmed by the civility and helpfulness of the cleaners. At least in this hospital it was *they* who apologized if they had to ask you to move to another area in order to wash the floor. I had come across some horrors elsewhere: staff who seemed to consider anyone daring to cross their path as hell bent on making their lives as difficult as possible. "I don't know why I bloody well bother," I heard one such charmer in Poole say after my craven apology. "I no sooner get the floor clean and someone's walking their shoes all over it." Clearly she expected me either to float above her or to delay my attendance on a patient until her floor had dried.

Our ward clerk too was quietly competent. She reminded me of Mrs Tiggy-Winkle, bustling about, checking the laundry room and the stationery cupboard, busy with her own business, but never too busy to help with ours. I always rather expected to find spines poking through the back of her white coat. Her filing was immaculate and her paperwork always up to date. She was a great source of information, both professional and personal.

"Mr Y [one of the consultants] is always on time for his ward round. If you are in charge on that morning, you need to be ready a few minutes before he's due. Make sure that any results from any tests are to hand in the front of the file. He gets very irritated if he has to shuffle through the notes to find them."

"Yes, Sister Seal has told me," I reassured her.

"You can't hear it too often, dear. By the way, Dr X, the new registrar, is very demanding I hear, quite the big man, but he's probably nervous, so we need to give him a week's grace."

"Don't waste your time on him, dear," she advised, when I sighed over a tall houseman who bore more than a passing resemblance to Paul McCartney. "He's going out very seriously with an auburn-haired sister on one of the gynae wards."

"How do you know?"

"I sat behind them in the cinema last week. He was all over her like a rash. Anyway, you're better off out of it; I don't think you can trust a man who wears yellow socks."

"What's wrong with yellow socks?"

"What's right with yellow socks? No taste, that's what's wrong. He's probably the kind of man who does up the bottom button of his waistcoat."

"Is that wrong too?"

"Very wrong, dear. Not morally wrong, but a real fashion faux pas."

I checked this piece of information the next time I met my father. He was adamant. "Sartorially it's a real no-no; the bottom button must always be left undone. Doing it up would be as bad as wearing grey shoes, or yellow socks for that matter." So that was that.

CHAPTER 15

A Flat, and a Cat called Jeremy

One afternoon I took a premature baby, snug and warm in its incubator but needing a little extra attention, up to the SCU on the top floor. We weren't very busy on A2 and after handing over the notes I stayed chatting for a few minutes to the senior sister, whom I had got to know. Looking out of the window and admiring the view, I noted the roof and castellation of a large grey brick and flint building beyond the hospital.

"It's Kingston Prison," she told me. "Mostly domestic killers, I believe; you know: wife killers. They brought a prisoner into outpatients the other day with a dreadful gash on his head. Fighting, I imagine. Who knows what goes on in there? He was quite young, nice looking too. He was handcuffed to his escort, a prison officer I think. Nobody made any attempt to hide the fact. I felt sorry for him. It seemed an unnecessary humiliation. There was a great fat copper there as well. I don't know where anyone thought he might go: the boy, I mean, not the copper. Actually," she added, looking at the notes I'd given her, "here's a funny thing. Talking of prisoners, this little mite's dad is in the clink. Did you know?"

"No. It wasn't my delivery. I was just asked to bring him up to you."

I stayed for a moment looking down at that grim place so close to us and yet so distant. We were surrounded, in the maternity unit, by life and hope; by happiness and a future. Across the road, there was grim restriction and unhappiness; probably sometimes despair, and undoubtedly an uncertain future. I thought of all the babies I had delivered. It is easy to believe that each one is a tiny blank canvas. But that's not true. Their genetic inheritance is fixed and so in the main is their family background. Who can tell the possible effects of the environment into which they will slot? Some will grow up well and happy, others not so. Accidents, disease, misfortune may lie in wait for any of them. Would one of my deliveries end up in thirty or so years' time across the road, handcuffed to a guard if they needed hospitalization? It was a sad thought. Was there a patron saint for prisoners? I thought St Jude or even St Rita, patron saint of lost causes and hopeless cases, might do, so offered up a hasty intercession. I discovered shortly afterwards that St Leonard is the patron saint of prisoners and, oddly, also the patron saint of women in labour! The church really does cover all eventualities.

I am not normally a great one for asking God, or indeed any of the saints, to intervene in our everyday affairs. I always feel it makes it all so arbitrary. If God answers one penitent's prayer but not another's, does it mean that one of them has prayed harder, with more faith or with more supplication, than the other? Does God say, "You should have prayed harder"? Or to misquote Richard the Third, "I'm not in the giving mood today"?

Prayer, I think, helps and comforts those who pray, puts them in touch with the divine, lifts them above the purely material and brings solace. Old nuns used to say to me, very gently, rather shocked by my view of the efficacy of prayer, "You are wrong, Sister Eleanor. God always answers our prayer, but maybe not the way we want or expect."

I found this the most exasperating response. "Look," I'd say, "if I am *really* thirsty and ask you for a drink of water, I don't want to be offered a glass of milk on the strength of it being what *you* think I need!"

And yet... and yet... I pray, have prayed and will pray, from a need to be heard. I believe that the Almighty cares about me and my affairs and concerns. As Isaiah says, I am precious in his eyes, and he knows me by my name (Isaiah 43:1–4).

After that sobering half hour I returned to the ward undoubtedly comforted. I also hoped St Rita or St Jude would keep an eye on the baby's father and on the young man with the gashed head.

After a month in the hospital accommodation we found a flat in Southsea, Portsmouth's seaside suburb, and moved in. The area was very pleasant. Salisbury Road ran parallel to the seafront, so the windows were south facing. The rent was inclusive, which was good but rather above what we could afford, so we invited another midwife from the hospital to join us. We didn't really know her very well and it was not a particularly successful match. It also meant that Di and I shared a bedroom. As neither of us wanted to share with a stranger, we had no option, and at least we had a bed each. So our third flatmate had the double room and Di and I were on the lower ground floor. The sitting room was sunny and elegant, with charming, comfortable, chintz-covered chairs. There was a good-sized kitchen-diner, a bathroom and a pretty little garden.

The elderly couple who owned the house lived above us. They were very pleasant and in time our landlady became positively motherly. Once, our vacuum cleaner broke and I asked to have it repaired. Mrs B said gently, "It has been dropped, you know. There's a big crack in the casing. We will get it repaired for you, but next time, should it happen again, we think you ought to pay for it."

I felt very ashamed, apologized penitently, and offered to pay on this occasion.

"No, no," she said. "You are all good girls. I'm sure it was an accident and I know you aren't paid very much. If you could just be a little more careful in future."

None of us knew who was the offender: nobody admitted to it. It was probably me, as I am clumsy to a fault.

Shortly after we moved in, an elegant and very determined cat, a large, lean tabby, began to appear on our doorstep. Our lease said "No pets", so initially we just stroked him. But he began to wait for us, sitting patiently on the little wall by the front door. No matter which of us turned up, and no matter at what time, there he was. The minute he espied us, he would flip onto his back and writhe seductively, waiting for his belly to be tickled. Inevitably, one day he followed me through the door, and once we began to feed him he moved in.

He was full of character and very vocal. He made himself completely at home in the flat. When it was sunny he would stretch full length in front of the window, basking in the warmth. He protested vociferously if anybody attempted to move him. Try as I might, I couldn't keep him out of the bedroom. At night I would hear him scratching at the door; in the end it was easier to let him in.

"He's like all men," I observed to Di. "He's hoping to wear us down with his persistence."

"Well, it's certainly working with you," she laughed.

My periods of night duty were bliss for him and for me. He would curl up in the small of my back and purr so loudly I expected him to explode. I suspected Di had him on her bed when it was her turn. I discovered just how much I had missed the company of animals over the previous ten years. I didn't count fat Bijou, the dog in Mary-Mount convent, who was an unattractive animal. As a child there had always been dogs and cats at home. The rules of my late congregation forbade keeping pets, but several convents had dogs, presumably on the grounds of protection for the community. They were invariably spoiled, overfed and under-exercised.

I never knew a convent to have a cat. Cats are sensual creatures, both to observe and to interact with. Possibly the writhing and stretching was too suggestive of the pleasure of human sexuality. The sheer enjoyment a cat finds in being caressed is so clearly an intense physical response; perhaps even the reciprocal reaction from a human is problematic. Certainly nobody seeing the almost exquisite pleasure and satisfaction a cat gets from playing with a mouse, and how the experience is often prolonged, could be in doubt that here is a creature relishing its sensuality. Our cat, with his slightly Siamese profile and his lean sinuous frame, couldn't get enough of human contact. This feline character was a charmer.

I don't know what T. S. Eliot would have made of him. His personality was less Macavity than Skimbleshanks, but he would probably have chosen for himself the character of the Rum Tum Tugger.

We were a little apprehensive about our landlords discovering this vagrant and made every effort to conceal his presence. We should have come clean, because they almost certainly knew, right from the word go. They must have seen him from their kitchen window at the back of the house, which overlooked the garden. Once, I arrived at the front door at the same time as our landlady. I pointedly ignored the cat, which was difficult to do, as he was twining himself around my legs, purring. She looked down and just gave a little smile. I fully expected her to come down that evening and insist on his departure, but nothing was said. A few days later I saw her husband bending down to stroke him outside the gate, so I felt we had a tacit agreement that we could keep him.

We never did discover where he had come from or who he belonged to. To all intents and purposes he belonged to us. We called him Jeremy, after a boy I went out with a couple of times in Chichester and who had the unnerving habit of turning up unexpectedly at the flat in Stockbridge Road, expecting to be fed and entertained, usually I believe because he had been let down by another girl and was at a loose end. Jeremy cat was sweeter, more attractive and certainly more loyal than his human counterpart.

Life in Portsmouth was good. We were extremely comfortable in Salisbury Road, loved the flat and relished entertaining, which became a regular occurrence. We spent hours dreaming up recipes and trying them out on our friends, though it would be more exact to say we tried them out on our girlfriends, for there continued, initially, to be a dearth of available men. Dinner parties were in vogue, and casual jeans and tee-shirt were not considered suitable evening wear. Fashion in the seventies is best described as "romantic". If men were suddenly embracing colour – paisley patterned shirts with big lapelled collars, kipper ties and pastel-tinted flared trousers – the girls saw Laura Ashley as the *sine qua non* of style. We entered a new Edwardian age of ankle-length, tight-waisted dresses, all flounces and frills and usually high at the neck, giving a demure and even modest appearance. Occasionally to give an "edge" to the ensemble the bolder teamed these charmingly feminine frocks with Doc Martin boots, the bigger and heavier the better. It was not a match that pleased me. I thought it made the wearer look like Popeye's Olive Oyl.

Much as I would have loved to possess Laura Ashley dresses, they were beyond the purse of an impecunious midwife, but I hit upon a solution that was as cheap as it was practical. Marks and Spencer did a very pretty line in full-length cotton nighties in lovely colours, and complete with the obligatory frills and lacy flounces. Two or three of those did me very well for a year or two as party and evening wear; eventually I put them to their proper use.

Some of the nurses went clubbing, an activity that had me bemused. Although I was assured by some of the more adventurous girls that "that's where the men are", I really couldn't feel enthusiastic about it. We tried the Pomme D'Or, a huge, noisy club in Palmerstone Road, but I found its frenetic activity very unappealing. I was still trying to catch up with the pop scene. In Chichester, Dee had encouraged us to watch *The Old Grey Whistle Test*, which she said was very cutting edge, but most of the music I found very prosaic, although I loved the Rolling Stones, and the Beatles continued to enchant me. Having rejected the Pomme D'Or, we tried other clubs: Nero's and Joanna's on the seafront, but they were even less appealing. What I disliked most about the club scene was the sheer volume of the music.

"It's so loud. It's impossible to talk, and the cost of a drink is extortionate." I was sitting in the ward office on my coffee break with Anthea Seal and a couple of housemen, and complaining about what I considered had been a wasted evening.

They all smiled at each other. "I don't think you've understood the club scene. One can hardly blame you, given your recent old life," said one of the doctors. By this time, my religious past was generally well known by my colleagues. "You don't go to clubs to talk, or to drink for that matter, although one invariably does end up at the bar, and yes I do agree the booze is expensive. You go to the clubs to dance and to listen to the music and to hang out with your friends."

"It's an odd atmosphere. There are people sitting in the gloom with sunglasses on! Some of the people I saw there yesterday evening looked as if they only appear at night. They are probably vampires or werewolves. They had a kind of unhealthy pallor as if they had just crawled out from under a stone. I never see people like that in the day time. Where do they go; where are they from? And what's with all the white suits and *clogs*?"

"I don't think the strobe lights help. Nobody looks normal under them," said Anthea. "But I agree with you; sunglasses, white suits and clogs is very bizarre."

A pleasanter experience was the Nuffield Club. My father, an ex-army officer, had taken me there on one of his visits. It was for officers from all the armed forces. There was a large bar and lounge and a lovely enclosed veranda overlooking Hampshire County Cricket Ground. Portsmouth was no longer a garrison town, so army officers were not well represented. It was, however, widely used by young naval officers who had no home in the city, wanted to escape from the wardroom in the evenings, or were passing through on leave and needed accommodation for one or more nights. Di and I became enthusiastic attenders.

Saturday nights were lively and we began to see the same faces regularly at the bar. It was a rather traditional sort of place, I suppose, befitting an officers' club. Someone would buy me a drink and then occasionally ask me out to dinner or the cinema. I remembered my experience in Chichester with a more mature man, and was determined not to be fooled again, so some of my new acquaintances were very startled when after a polite "How do you do" or an informal "Hi" I would ask baldly, "Are you married?"

I was dismayed to find how many of them were. I did have a mild flirtation with a naval dentist, but it remained a very platonic affair. He had a girlfriend in Guildford whom he expected to marry, so nothing was going to come of our friendship, but it was a pleasant interlude. He was intelligent and good company, but there was no spark and we parted on affable terms when he was posted to Chatham.

CHAPTER 16

A Brother's Recommendation

The large expanse of green parkland between the sea and Southsea was called the Common. Ladies Mile, a long avenue running diagonally across it, was once lined with trees, but Dutch Elm disease put paid to that. The holm oaks that were also a feature of the Common were not affected. Many of these trees had an odd shape due to the strength of the prevailing south-easterly winds. The tops, rather than being dome shaped, tended to bend to the north as if a large hand was squashing them down; they resembled old ladies with their heads bowed, struggling against the elements.

A half-mile walk along the seafront and then a cut across the Common brought me to my brother's place in Nightingale Road. He shared a flat with Linda his fiancée and a fierce black tom cat, a real Macavity, who terrorized all other cats in the area. He was probably the only animal to survive feline flu, due to Linda's tender and diligent care, even wiping his nose! He would sit on the high, stone gate post by their door and glower threateningly at everyone, occasionally giving a swipe with his paw, claws out, at anybody foolish enough to pass too close.

Peter was at teacher training college in Twickenham, but came home at the weekend. On Sundays, if I wasn't on duty, I took to meeting him, and sometimes Linda, at a tiny and very hospitable pub called The Blacksmith's Arms, known as "The Blackies". It is now covered by Waitrose supermarket – great for parking, but you can't get beer on tap any more! Sitting in the bar of The Blackies was rather like sitting in someone's front room. It was small, warm, intimate and a little shabby, with the shiny shabbiness that comes from things that are well used but well loved.

"I recommend the kipper rolls; they're the best in town." Peter seemed very firm about this. I wasn't in any position to argue, but I felt I needed to know more about Portsmouth's reputation for kippers.

"Whatever do you mean? Is Portsmouth known for its kipper rolls, like Eccles for cakes, or Bakewell for tarts, or Chelsea for buns, or Bath for Olivers, whatever they are? Anyway, I don't like kippers. They repeat on me and I can taste them for days."

"You'll like these, I promise."

He was clearly bent on encouraging me, so I gave in and they were very good. Doris, the landlady, prepared them by the simple expedient of standing them upright in a jug and pouring boiling water over them. She let them stand for about two minutes, then fished them out and slapped them between two halves of a roll. There was a complete absence of kipper smell and they didn't repeat on me.

I was delighted to see Peter so regularly. In the eighteen months since I had been in Portsmouth we had seen each other often. My relationship with him was a source of great comfort and pleasure. He was four years my junior and when he was barely a year old, I had been packed off to boarding school. When I eventually left this convent school and became a day girl elsewhere, he was still only six, so playing together was not very exciting. We began to interact more immediately in Hong Kong. My father was posted there in 1955 and in due course we followed him. The outdoor life, the beach, the picnics, the intimacy of life in a flat with only a balcony or tiny garden to play in, drew us together. It all changed again on our return to England. Peter went first to prep and then to public school; he was miserable at both. I missed him terribly but we spent time together in the holidays: rode out on our bikes, walked the dogs or went to the cinema. He became very good company; witty, fun and very non-confrontational. As I was older and certainly bossier, he usually gave in to my suggestions about our leisure time together.

When I announced to my parents my plans for entering a convent, I got very stern advice from my father as to how I should break this bombshell to my brother. My father, who was singularly thick-skinned himself and almost totally devoid of empathy, was sure that my brother, whom he declared was sensitive, would take the announcement very badly. I was astonished: not about my brother's sensitivity, which I knew all about, but by my father's apparent awareness of it. It certainly wasn't reflected in his treatment of his son. He was not a particularly harsh disciplinarian, although both of us had felt his hand on more than one occasion – in fact he was affectionate – but he seemed oblivious or even indifferent to our deeper needs.

Having taken his advice to heart, however, I told Peter rather tentatively one afternoon that I would be leaving home to go to France to enter a convent, with the view to becoming a nun. I had chosen the garden for this disclosure so that if he cried or raged, he wouldn't be overheard by either of our parents. He looked very serious and was quiet for a minute or two, kicking a stone around in a desultory way. Eventually he lifted his head and looked steadily at me. I wondered whatever was coming and waited apprehensively. Then he said, "Are you going to take your yellow leather jacket with you or your green silk scarf? If not, can I have them?" So much for teenage angst!

Peter came out to France twice during my time as a novice and, on each occasion, I thought him more handsome and more charming. He wowed the sisters, both in France, showing my novice mistress how to dance the twist, and in Liverpool. The elderly nuns thought him a "dote" and spoiled him. Years later, tongue in cheek I hope, he said that my decision to become a nun had always mystified him, despite seeing how happy I was, until he guessed or assumed that I was working undercover for MI6.

My rediscovery of him as an adult was a joy. He seemed very self-assured, very confident – a cover for a degree of uncertainty that I was to see later. He could also be obstinate, a characteristic that persisted. I tried once, years later, to persuade him to try skiing. He was very fit and a keen distance runner.

"Why don't you try skiing? You'd love it. All that fresh air and beautiful scenery; it's wonderful."

"No. I know I wouldn't like it."

"You would; *you would*, and you'd pick it up so quickly."

"Eleanor, sweetie, I know I wouldn't like it."

"How can you say that? You haven't tried it. Honestly, it's amazing."

"I wouldn't like it. I *know* I wouldn't like it."

No reason at all. Not "I don't like snow – I hate being cold" or even "I only do things I'm sure I am going to be good at". Just a bald "I know I wouldn't like it". I gave up. There was no point in kicking against a stone. Part of me was irritated, but part of me admired his certainty about what he wanted or didn't want.

We were sitting outside The Blackies one lunchtime having a drink. I felt blissfully happy in his company, and looked at him, smiling.

"What?" he said. "*What?*"

"Nothing; really, nothing." I kept smiling but looked away. How can you tell a brother the depth of your love for him? It seemed so un-British, not very Anglo-Saxon, so perhaps the Gallic influence from those years in France was still very strong in me. Nuns didn't do it, but elsewhere in France people were always throwing their arms around each other. A handshake is a cool, professional greeting. Fathers and sons, brothers and male friends, embraced with enthusiasm. Women kissed each other on both cheeks and children put up their faces and puckered their lips with complete spontaneity. I wanted to throw my arms around my little brother, right there in public, and hug him. I kept my voice light. "You're very hairy these days." His thick brown hair was long and he sported a *Viva Zapata!* moustache.

"Yep, I'm sorry. It's the fashion." He got up. "Come on, I'll teach you how to play pool." He set up the rack on the table and picked up a cue.

I tried hard but I wasn't very good; I have poor hand-to-eye coordination.

"I'll let you win," I said generously.

"OK," he agreed, grinning, then deftly knocking the last ball into the pocket queried, "How's your social life these days?"

I just laughed. It was a prescient question, as he knew all about my chequered career. I was dating, off and on, a young man in the Fleet Air Arm. It was a very unsatisfactory relationship. Most of my friends disliked him, and I wondered whether I didn't rather dislike him myself. I was never quite sure why, but there was something a bit "off-centre" about him. He was divorced and once let drop that he had been brought up in a children's home. He had a child too, a little girl who lived with his ex-wife in Dundee, and whom he saw rarely. He was terrifyingly right wing, even for someone in a profession that itself is quite noticeably right of centre. He was far from being my ideal partner, despite his fair good looks. His commanding officer warned me off him, saying bluntly, "You think you'll raise him up, but you won't. He'll drag you down." I was astonished at such a direct remark, but he added, "I've got a daughter a little younger than you, and I would be horrified if she got tangled up with someone like him."

Eventually I dropped him. My elusive soul mate was still evading me.

"Why do you waste your time with these people?" Peter and Linda had come to supper. There was some bitterness in Peter's voice, his tongue loosened by several glasses of Valpolicella. His memories of our family life, dominated by the army, made him singularly unsympathetic to having a sister involved with any aspect of the services. "Do you *want* to be a naval wife? Haven't you had enough of service life? Continually on the move, living in ghastly married quarters; all that struggle to advance your husband's career; all that endless standing around at cocktail parties making small talk to people you don't know or don't like and who have nothing interesting to say?"

I was taken aback by his vehemence, and an uneasy silence fell. Di was defensive.

"Some of the men we meet at the Nuffield Club are very nice, charming, intelligent, good company. You talk as if all service personnel are morons. I know plenty of doctors who don't appear ever to have read a book, if you are going to talk about narrow intellect. What do you think?" Her question was addressed to Linda.

"I don't know any doctors socially, and I don't know anybody in the services except Peter's father. He seems quite OK, a bit jolly and blustery perhaps, but I haven't had any lengthy, or what one might call intellectual, conversations with him. He does read books though; he's very keen on Jeffrey Archer."

When Linda compressed her lips to hide a smile, two deep dimples appeared in her cheeks and this disingenuous comment produced just such a result. Di attempted to defuse the situation by serving coffee and yet more Valpolicella.

"We'll find someone one day; no rush," she said breezily.

"I tell you what," said Peter, returning to the fray. "I know this guy; Linda and I lodged with him for a bit before getting the flat. You'd love him, he's great! He's intelligent and witty, in a sardonic kind of way, but he's really nice, and well read too. He's got a sports car and his own house. He's got a great job – he works for IBM – so he's probably well off too. Oh, and he's tall. Honestly, he's so right for you."

"You haven't told me what he looks like or how old he is, this paragon."

"I don't know, about twenty-six or seven I suppose. It's difficult to tell. He's got a beard."

"A beard!" I yelped. "Peter, for heaven's sake! I don't want some hairy giant. You'll tell me next he wears socks with sandals!"

No more was said about Peter's hairy friend, either that evening or in the following weeks.

The summer seemed to end swiftly. By mid-September a week of strong wind made for an unexpectedly early autumn, and leaves, piled high in great red and brown drifts on the Common, crunched under my feet. We had a sudden frost and the bonnet of Di's car was covered in something that looked like chilly icing sugar. Jeremy cat was very reluctant to leave the house and we had to be firm with him. In October the clocks went back, the evenings were dark and it was too cold to sit outside pubs.

Inside The Blackies' snug front room, the windows ran with condensation as we chatted and drank, oblivious to the blue fug of cigarette smoke, but cosseted by the warm friendly ambience.

Across the Solent, the Isle of Wight was shrouded in sea mist and in the evening the lights of Ryde glimmered dimly, surrounded by a ghostly aura. The brown sea was choppy, the waves crested with beige foam, so only intrepid sailors ventured out. The wind on the front was sometimes strong enough to buffet those foolhardy enough to risk a walk. On particularly fierce days it was closed to traffic, as showers of pebbles could be flung inland even as far as the Common. But the flat was lovely and cosy and we were toasty warm. Portsmouth seemed a friendly, homely place; Poole just a bad memory.

As in previous years, the Christmas displays in the shop windows affronted me. "It's not even Advent yet; we've got Halloween beforehand," I grumbled. Christmas cards were on sale the minute the school holidays were over, followed shortly after by wrapping paper covered with fat snowmen, jolly Santas and dyspeptic-looking reindeer.

Promptly, as if they understood my irritation, Linda and Peter put a card through our door inviting us to come to supper on 31 October and enjoy the eve of All Saints with baked potatoes and mulled wine. They had recently moved to a small house, still in Southsea but back from the seafront. It was an end of terrace, and benefited from a walled courtyard that looked as if it might well be a suntrap in the summer; they called it, with deliberate irony, Dingly-Dell.

Their sitting room was very welcoming. There was a briskly burning fire and red candles in raffia-covered wine bottles placed strategically if rather hazardously round the room. This fashion, which seems so dated now, was considered *de rigueur* at the time and thought to be the very essence of rakish and bohemian chic; it was actually reassuringly cosy.

There seemed an inordinate crowd of people gathered in such a small space, but it was cheerfully noisy. Peter greeted me affectionately and thrust a glass of something hot, red, sticky and spicy into my hand. I squeezed out into the hall looking for somewhere to sit, feeling a bit lost. In the dim light it was difficult to distinguish faces, and anyway apart from Di, Peter and Linda I didn't know a soul. Eventually I found myself perching on the stairs next to a fair-haired, good-looking man who made a place for me, patting the stair and introducing himself with easy cheerfulness as Ed. "That's my wife Annie," he said, indicating a large, tall, pleasant-faced girl in animated conversation with a group by the door. I began to relax and enjoy myself. It was all very convivial and I anticipated a good boozy evening.

"How do you know my brother?" I asked him.

"Peter and Linda stayed in *my* brother's house before they moved to Southsea, so I got to know them quite well. My brother's here somewhere." He looked around vaguely. "He'd forgotten about this party, so we just dragged him out. I think he's still got his slippers on."

As the evening wore on, other people turned up and some left, and by midnight the crowd had reduced to about a dozen people and there was room for me in the sitting room, on a worn but comfortable sofa. Conversation became general and turned to a television programme recently aired, about the art treasures in the Vatican. There were quite vehement views expressed about the morality of the church acquiring and then hanging on to such a valuable collection.

"If only a few were sold, there would be enough money to feed all the beggars and homeless in Rome for a year."

I craned my neck to see who had voiced this suggestion, but failed to identify the speaker. There was a murmur of agreement. Some part of me was sympathetic to this opinion, but perversely I felt, as I always do when "outsiders" criticize the church, that I should defend it. I was, for all I knew, the only representative Catholic in the room, and the part of devil's advocate, in an inverse sort of way, fell to me.

"The Vatican treasures are not for the personal use of the Holy Father," I said. "You are talking as if he was King Midas, or do I mean Croesus? Well, never mind. I'm sure he has other things to do than count his millions and drape himself in priceless tapestries while admiring Fra Angelico's paintings. The Vatican is a museum; these treasures belong to the church." I began to warm to my theme, and continued heatedly, "They are there for anybody to see and admire. You don't suggest that the British Museum should sell its art collection to realize funds to give down-and-outs in London a roof over their head, do you? The Pope is just a curator."

A slightly embarrassed hush fell and then a sleepy and rather ironic voice from a dim corner of the room said soothingly, "Never mind, my dear. I'm sure he's a dear old pope anyway."

This sally was greeted by a burst of laughter that I joined in with. But my curiosity was aroused and under cover of accepting another drink and lighting a cigarette, I peered myopically at the vague shape from which the voice had emanated. I was aware of a rather bizarre figure who, as far as the dim light allowed me to see, appeared to be wearing an orange rugby shirt, a rather worn pair of what looked like lime green cords and slippers. His face remained in shadow and I sensed rather than saw that he was smiling. I chose to ignore him and not to respond to this remark.

Back in the flat I asked Di, "Who was that strange fellow that made such an odd remark about the Pope? You know, when they were all talking about the Vatican treasures."

"I don't know what his name is, but I think he's the brother of that nice guy with the big wife... Ed? They're nice, aren't they, Ed and Annie? What I can tell you is that the guy in the corner was the chap your brother thinks is your perfect partner."

I could only stare at her in astonished disbelief. "Peter must be mad! He's some sort of bearded weirdo."

"Ed and Annie seem nice and normal; maybe he's just eccentric. Every family should have one. Maybe he'll grow on you." I could see she was laughing at me.

"As I haven't the slightest intention of having anything to do with him, I think it unlikely that he'll grow on me, as you put it."

A couple of days later, returning home from work, I picked up a scrappy note addressed to me lying on the mat outside the door. Puzzled, I turned it over a couple of times, scrutinizing it dubiously. I thought it was a joke. I had never seen such an ill-formed hand and thought it had been written by a child. "Would you like to meet for a drink? I'll catch you on the electric string. Dick."

"It's the weirdo," said Di. "I met him on the steps. He was just leaving. He said he'd left a note. He seemed quite nice and pretty normal, as far as I could tell. No carpet slippers this time – a suit and tie."

Two days later Peter phoned me at work. "See you in The Blackies Sunday lunchtime, if you are free. I know you're starting a week of night duty."

I found my brother standing at the bar, and beside him, smiling pleasantly, a large, tall man with a thick black beard. *The weirdo*, I thought. Weirdo or not, his smile was warm and attractive. His beard didn't hide a full mouth and a curling bottom lip that gave his face a rather satyr-like appearance. Although I didn't think him handsome, there was something of the antique Greek sculpture about his head that I thought rather appealing. His eyes, behind thick-rimmed glasses, were an unusual light brown. He was quietly spoken – a listener rather than a talker, I thought. I was a little embarrassed, as I hadn't responded to his note, and mumbled something about meaning to get back to him. Peter called him Dick, which I assumed was short for Richard.

"We don't have a phone in the flat," I explained, "and I didn't have your number."

"That's fine. Maybe when you've finished night duty. I'll leave another note." He smiled his warm smile again and I thought, *Uhmm. Yes, why don't you do that!* and smiled back. There were no sardonic remarks about the Pope either.

CHAPTER 17

Nights – July 1972

I had always liked night duty. My body clock adapted quickly and in general I had no problem sleeping during the day. Even the raucous voices and grinding mechanism of the dustbin lorries or school children passing the house failed to disturb me, though both of my flatmates complained bitterly about external noise. With Jeremy cat curled up beside me, and a hot water bottle at my feet if it was cold, I usually managed a good seven hours' unbroken slumber.

At the hospital also, the atmosphere was different. There was something about the intimacy in the ward that wasn't evident during the day. Perhaps it was the curtained windows and the darkness beyond that made us feel secluded and sheltered, in our own warm little world. The staff seemed more relaxed and the integration between the various professional levels closer. On night duty there were more part-time midwives and a higher proportion of auxiliary nurses. Both these groups were often older women who had returned to work after raising their own families. I undoubtedly benefited from their professional experience.

Night duty could be challenging, though. From 2 to 4 a.m., if we were not busy, we became almost lightheaded with a sort of disembodied fatigue. This period always seemed to me the hardest time. It was often difficult to stay awake. I found that, just as in Broadgreen when I was on night duty, confidences that would have been suppressed in the cold light of day were shared with intemperate recklessness, particularly in the small hours. Here the secrets openly shared were from the nurses, not the patients. Women together, I learned, will almost inevitably reveal details of the most personal relationships: parent–child, husband–wife. It would only take one to begin, and almost competitively others would join in. Sometimes, in fact mostly, it was funny and rarely bitter or recriminatory. It was, I suppose, a release mechanism on their part – glad to get it out of their system in this strange half-life. A nursing auxiliary, who often gave me a lift home, seemed to have a perfectly charming and affectionate husband, and yet we were regularly entertained by a hilarious and not altogether kind account of his qualities and defects both as a man and a husband.

My colleagues were also sometimes astoundingly revelatory about their health. Illnesses and operations were discussed with graphic detail, and not just their own but their partners'. We were prone to uncontrollable laughter on occasions. This relaxed and casual atmosphere was replicated in the adaptation we made to our uniform. Cardigans and shawls made their appearance, although these would be taken off when we went to attend to our charges. Sometimes our caps and aprons were removed, and it wasn't uncommon for some of the older women to put on slippers. This would never have been tolerated at any of my Liverpool hospitals, but even the senior night sister at St Mary's didn't bat an eyelid.

On quiet nights we could read or knit; sometimes we played cards or just chatted in the little sitting room next to the office. At meal breaks, few of us bothered to walk all the way over to the canteen, but preferred to bring in a snack or a sandwich. Sometimes someone would bring in a cake, which we would fall upon and devour with endless cups of coffee. More than one of us existed the entire six days on crisps and chocolate biscuits. Some people maintained that they gained half a stone in the six or seven nights on; others lost weight. We would have done better to have eaten normally, just reversing the timetable, but most couldn't face cereal or porridge or even coffee and toast at 5 p.m., nor a full lunch at 1 a.m., so we "grazed".

Some of us developed odd culinary tastes. In Liverpool it was the ubiquitous chip butty: thick chips sandwiched between two well-buttered slices of white bread. Certainly the carbohydrates gave us energy. What it did to our waist line was problematic. My own yearning, when on nights in Portsmouth, was for a pastry that would have no appeal at all for me during ordinary daytime work periods. I often passed a little bakery on my way home, and, lured inside by the hot luscious odour of fresh bread and the buttery smell of croissants, would buy two Eccles cakes. One I ate as I walked along. The taste was heavenly. My mother would have been horrified. She considered eating in the street to be the height of vulgarity. The second I would plan to take into work with me that night. Sometimes I weakened and ate it lying in bed, only to wake up with my pillow covered in crumbs and the guilty realization that I had gone to sleep without brushing my teeth.

Most of us on nights complained of feeling bloated. This was unsurprising, given the irregularity and the peculiarity of our diet. On one occasion, one of the girls brought in a box of fondant fancies. I didn't particularly like them but they were greeted with rapture by the others, who fell on them with glee. Two of us went off to do the baby feeds, leaving the others to gorge. Afterwards, coming into the sitting room, I took off my apron, stained with milk and other unmentionables, kicked off my shoes and sank down into an armchair, then stiffened in alarm.

I had recently acquired contact lenses. They were very comfortable and I was delighted to escape from the glasses that my vanity found less than acceptable. The lenses were hard, gas permeable, and a replacement was moderately expensive. On night duty my eyes tended to become dry, and it only needed an inauspicious swipe or bump, and a lens would flick out. In taking off my apron, I had inadvertently swept the corner across my face and dislodged one.

"What's the matter?" said the plump, always reliable auxiliary nurse sitting opposite me.

"I've lost a contact lens; it's just flipped out."

"Don't move! Where do you think it is?" She was up in a flash.

"I don't know. Oh, be careful; you might tread on it! Can anybody see it on my dress? It could be anywhere. Oh, damn. The other day this happened and it had flipped down the neck of my blouse and was in my bra!"

One of the difficulties was the concave shape of the lens. If it fell with the domed side up, it could be spotted more easily, as light reflected off the surface. If it fell the other way, there wasn't much chance of finding it. Also because of its shape it tended to spin, so could be a foot or more away. We all sat staring at the floor for a moment and then I stood up cautiously. Several hands began patting me down gently.

"It's no good," said my auxiliary friend, taking off her cardigan and thereby metaphorically rolling up her sleeves. "You'd better take your dress off and we can search it properly."

I stood meekly as I was divested of my dress, my companions going carefully over the material. Standing in my bra and pants, I peered hopefully down at my cleavage and saw only what one usually expects to see in a bra. I raised my arms and squinted along them. Nothing!

There was a discreet cough and we all looked up. Standing in the doorway, with an expression on his face in which astonishment and embarrassment were equally mixed, was the duty houseman. I was so anxious about my lost lens that I doubt if I even blushed, although the tableau must have been extraordinary: four women, three of them wearing an assortment of non-standard nurse's uniform and a fourth in bra and pants but with her nurse's cap still firmly pinned to her head.

"Is there a problem?" he asked solemnly.

"Yes, there is. We are all looking for my contact lens," I babbled. "But we haven't found it."

"I'd offer to help," he said, "but I don't think I should. Perhaps I can have a cake to help me on my way. I've had a busy, busy night on A4." He eyed the fondant fancies, reached into the box and took one. With the cake halfway to his mouth, he paused. "Is this what you are looking for?"

Perched on top of a sugar violet like a tiny frisbee was my contact lens. He blenched and put the cake down. "I don't think I want this now. I could have swallowed your lens."

"Don't worry: your stomach acid would have dissolved it. Please excuse me." I summoned up some dignity. "I want to get dressed now."

He disappeared, giving me what my mother would have called "an old-fashioned stare". The rest of the night was uneventful until, as often happened, two mothers who had laboured tranquilly through the night went into second stage at 6 a.m. I was an hour late getting home, and there had been a run on Eccles cakes, so I had to make do with an iced bun.

We were not always quiet. There is an ongoing argument about the proportion of babies born during the night as opposed to those born during daylight hours. In the present millennium, when the rate of elective caesarean births is steadily rising and more labours are induced, there are almost certainly more daytime deliveries, but in the seventies a surprisingly large number of women in labour arrived in the small hours, and consequently night duty was often a time of high activity.

Fewer and fewer women were breastfeeding, and at night the babies were fed by the nursing staff so their mothers could get a decent sleep. Even the breast-fed babies would be changed and wrapped up before being brought quietly to their sleepy parent. We had to be vigilant, though. Some women who had had other babies and were old hats at childbirth would drop off to sleep while suckling their child. I was always scared that dropping off to sleep might have, as a consequence, a dropping off of their baby from a high hospital bed onto an unforgiving hospital floor. It never happened, but I always liked to keep an eye open and an ear out for anything untoward.

It was on night duty that I had two of the saddest experiences in my life as a midwife. A young woman expecting her first baby was admitted in strong labour late one evening. Her waters had broken and her underwear and pad were stained with a brown discharge, indicating that all was not well. Babies in distress in the womb often defecate and this produces stained amniotic fluid.

Despite listening carefully, I could hear no foetal heartbeat. Normally, with a live child, the womb has a symphony of its own. The heartbeat is rapid, sometimes described as "galloping", and rather staccato. Behind it, the foetal cord has a ghostly, low, resonating, whooshing howl, poetically described as "the sound of the wind over the Romney marshes". The two sounds interact with each other like reassuring if dissonant chords. This womb was silent.

She told me she hadn't felt the baby move that day. In fact, the baby's movements hadn't been very noticeable for a day or two. "Just the odd little flutter," she said. After what was thankfully a fairly short labour I delivered a stillborn baby, a little boy.

This was my first experience of what is called a fresh stillbirth, a full-term child who inexplicably dies just before or during labour. Had she come into the unit the previous day with any problem, she could have been delivered by caesarean, but the poor girl had no reason to think anything was wrong, and she had no experience to warn her that reduced movement at term might indicate something serious. I had seen stillbirths before; premature babies too frail to survive the rigours of labour or those born with serious genetic defects. Often the babies carried by severely diabetic mothers did not survive the forty weeks of uterine life and died some weeks before their term. But this incident was a new experience for me and one that I found very distressing.

I looked at the baby lying on the scales in the sluice; even stillborns have to be weighed. I couldn't believe that it was impossible to breathe some life into him. He was absolutely perfect, a beautiful child, his flesh still firm. How could he be so flawless and so dead? The afterbirth was "gritty", the granular deposits of calcification indicating quite evidently a placental insufficiency, which would appear to be the only explanation for this unexpected and tragic occurrence. We were all very gentle with the young couple and they went home very sorrowfully some hours later.

The second event involved a baby whose defects had been diagnosed by amniocentesis, a withdrawal of the fluid around the baby while in the womb. He had a severe spina bifida, a congenital defect of the spinal column and cord. The parents had been told and so knew the outcome. The mother was admitted in strong labour in the early hours. I never heard a sound from her. Each contraction was a mountain that she climbed with a grim determination not to admit her suffering or despair. She gritted her teeth and sweated in silence. It was unnerving. When her child was delivered, she turned her face away. He was wrapped in a blanket and taken up to the special baby care unit without her or her husband seeing him.

I was very weary – it had been a hard night – but before going home I went up to the unit to see the baby. The open lesion down the spine was evident and quite clearly inoperable, but he was a pretty baby with a shock of black hair, peaceful and asleep.

"It's just a matter of time really," the sister told me. "He's been sedated and if he cries we'll feed him, but the outlook is inevitable."

I went slowly and thoughtfully back down to the ward and into the single room where the young couple were still wrapped in a terrible despairing silence. The girl sat in a chair, her husband holding her limp hand in his as he gazed blankly out of the window. One of my colleagues was making up the bed. The room was thick with tension and grief.

Hesitantly I said, "Listen, I may be talking out of turn and you must do as you wish, but I think you ought to know that you haven't given birth to something dreadful, to a monster, to a ghastly defect, to something too hideous to look at. You have a lovely baby upstairs. A baby who, sadly, we know is not able to survive, but who is beautiful; your child. I really do feel that you should go and see him."

The other midwife looked up sharply, her eyes narrowed. She frowned a little and gave a barely perceptible shake of her head. The young parents looked at me. I drew a breath and ignored the silent signal from across the room. "If you don't do this, your baby will never have felt his mother's touch. Don't you think he has the right to that?"

I knew I was on dangerous ground here. We were not encouraged to engage in this sort of emotional interaction; it was always deprecated. I knew what I was doing would not meet with overall approval, possibly quite the contrary. My colleague was red with what I thought might be confused embarrassment or maybe just acute disapproval.

"Well," I said lamely, "I don't mean to upset you." I slipped away wondering if I would be reported for inappropriate behaviour.

Next night when I arrived on duty I was told they had been to see the baby and held him; I was glad.

Thirty-five years later, shopping in Chichester for an outfit for a wedding, a charming and smiling sales assistant of about my age said, "You don't remember me, do you? But I've never forgotten you. You told me to go and hold my baby. Without you I would always have thought I'd given birth to a monstrosity. It was such a kind thing to do. We went to see him every day. He died very quickly, five days later, but he was our baby. We gave him a name and had him christened. We were so grateful to you."

I thought afterwards that this was one of the loveliest things that had ever happened to me.

CHAPTER 18

A Courtship

Night duty was followed by a rest period. Five nights off after seven nights on. Actually it was five nights and five days off. It took more than a few hours to readjust; for the world, as it were, to stop rotating in the opposite direction, to slow down and settle back on its axis. The days stretched ahead like eternity, and felt, each time, like the beginning of a new life; as if one had re-entered the world of the living. I always felt I should be doing something really novel and exciting; I never did. It was like living in a vacuum, all that empty time. Indeed the main problem for a young unmarried woman was to know how to fill it. A wife or mother would re-enter her domestic sphere and pick up the reins of her family life, but for the singleton it was different. Other acquaintances, nurses or not, were working, and getting a weekend as part of one's off-duty depended on the ward roster, so nights off during the working week were not much fun.

I went into Brighton to see my mother sometimes, occasionally staying the night, which meant sleeping on her sofa. Happily, they were cosy, cheerful meetings. Trips to Oxford to see my father, however, involved a long and expensive train journey. He came to Portsmouth two or three times a year to see his old drinking buddies, so we were in close touch.

I did a lot of reading during my nights off. For a while I had a great passion for Howard Spring and in a year read everything he ever wrote. Some of his stuff was real tear-jerking material. My flatmates would sometimes come home to find me huddled on the sofa, Jeremy cat on my lap, red-eyed and puffy-faced from a surfeit of *My Son, My Son* or, my favourite, *These Lovers Fled Away*. In the main, though, nights off were lonely and sometimes boring.

One spell ended with a weekend. I had left it too late to organize anything with other friends from the hospital for the Saturday. So I felt at a loose end.

"Have you got any plans for today?" Di was getting ready for work.

"Yes, actually." I had been thinking about what I was going to do since waking up. I looked at my watch: 10:15 a.m. I got out of bed. "I'm going to have a bath, wash my hair, then go up the road and ring Dick Richardson to see if he'd like to have a drink with me."

I had continued to bump into him occasionally with my brother. He always seemed pleased to see me, although the promised phone call had never materialized.

Di gazed at me with astonishment, dismay written all over her face. "You can't do that!"

"Why not?"

"You just can't. You can't just go round asking men out. You've got to wait for them to ask you. That's how it's done."

"Not today!" I felt rather giddy with the daringness of it all.

"But he'll think you are after him."

"I am after him. Look, I'll know, won't I? If he hesitates, or says he's busy or has other things to do, then I'll know that he's not interested. I haven't got anything to lose."

She shrugged and turned away, her disapproval very evident. I knew the score. Girls had to wait to be asked out. It wasn't done to seem too keen or too interested. You had to play it cool, to keep them guessing. It certainly wasn't acceptable to reverse the roles and become the hunter or, more correctly, the huntress.

The nearest pay phone was fifty yards up the road, so I hitched up my nightie, pulled on a pair of shoes and flung a coat around me, hoping that I wouldn't meet anybody I knew. At the telephone box my determination weakened for a moment, then I lifted the receiver and dialled his number. It rang for so long I nearly put the phone down. Then I heard his quiet pleasant voice. I took a deep breath and hoped my voice wouldn't shake at my audacity.

"Hi! It's Eleanor Stewart, Peter's sister. I'm off today, just finished nights, back on days tomorrow. I just wondered if you would like to meet me for a drink, at The Blackies perhaps?"

There was a longish pause. It was probably only about three seconds, but to my anxious ear it felt like five minutes. There was a slight element of something that might have been surprise in his response, although he told me later that he had been smiling.

"Love to. I'll pick you up in about forty minutes?"

"Yes, that would be great. Thanks." I hoped I sounded cool.

I raced back to the flat. "I've got a date," I said, "and something to do today, with a nice man." Di continued to look disapproving.

He was as good as his word. The doorbell rang as I was pulling on my boots.

Outside I saw his dark green Sunbeam Alpine, a sporty little two-seater roadster. This description was given to me later by a knowledgeable friend. I just saw an open-top sports car and grinned with pleasure. He looked rather dubiously at my light jacket; he was wearing the shabbiest duffle coat I'd ever seen. It was early December, but one of those unexpectedly warmish, sunny days

"You'll need a coat and a scarf. I thought I'd take a chance with the car and leave the top off, but it is December. It may rain. Shall we risk it?"

"Depends where we're going."

"I think we'll risk it," he said firmly. "If it rains, we'll just have to stay in the pub all afternoon."

The Red Lion at Chalton was enchanting. It was alleged to be the oldest pub in Hampshire: a glorious timber-framed building, with a thatched, moss-covered roof nearly reaching the ground at the east end and wonderful views across the rolling countryside down toward the Solent. Inside, a fire blazed in the inglenook. The place smelled of pine. Everything was burnished and glowing, and the Christmas decorations were lavish.

There seemed to be an amazing choice of beer and cider, and behind the bar was an array of fruit wines varying in colour from dark green (greengage) to purple (damson). I am always a little doubtful about so-called country wines. My view is that wine is made from grapes, but I had to admit the bottles looked pretty and, judging by the quantity left in most of them, very popular. I had a glass of apricot wine and then an elderflower, both of which were delicious but rather too sweet for my taste.

We sat and talked with ease. It was relaxed and curiously intimate, considering we hardly knew each other. He told me about himself: his inglorious naval career that he described with the irony that I was soon to become familiar with. Dartmouth Naval College was followed by three years of teaching junior seamen – years that he considered wasted. He hadn't enjoyed it and he didn't believe the boys had benefited.

The service ethos, so dear to my father's heart, was completely foreign to him. When I asked him why he had joined, he said that despite going to Southampton University with a Major Open Scholarship, his degree results had been so disappointing he couldn't think what else to do. At university he had discovered beer, girls and motorbikes, or any combination of the three, and frittered away his time. The navy was a job and he got board and lodgings. He felt, in retrospect, he'd paid a high price for it. Once, he told me, standing in a queue to see the Medical Officer, he was reading a book to while away the time and the tedium, and was very nearly put on a charge by some overenthusiastic senior officer. He rather liked the idea, he said, that a book could be seen as a fault against the Naval Discipline Act. Subversive, obviously! He had made some good friends despite it all, in the main as iconoclastic and non-conformist as he was.

IBM suited him better. He admired and respected his boss, the man who had recruited him, and he had pleasant colleagues whose intellect was stimulating. IBM was building new and powerful computers in the seventies – computers that were physically so huge that today they would fill a large garage. The microchip was as yet undreamed of. He said he was busy at work but that in the main he found life generally stressful. I remembered that Peter had told me he had some property and asked him about it. I was stunned to discover that he owned three houses, two of them in Carmarthen Avenue. This was a very sought-after residential road abutting the common land of the Portsdown hill. It seemed impolite to ask him about all this property but he volunteered the information that the houses were no problem; it was keeping the tenants happy and making sure they paid their rent on time that wore him out.

He asked me general questions about my tastes and my job, and didn't question me about my convent life, for which I was grateful. I imagine my brother had painted the general picture. As we drove back into Portsmouth, it began to rain a little and it became clear that we were not going to be able to enjoy the picnic he had prepared al fresco. Back home he produced a basket from the boot of the car and smiled a little diffidently as he showed it to me. Later he told me it constituted the entirety of his food shopping for the weekend. We spread the feast out on a tablecloth on the sitting room floor: a cold chicken, pâté, coleslaw, a baguette, some very ripe brie and a bottle of wine. The meal was delicious, and I was impressed and charmed by his ability to rise to the occasion. In The Blackies I had thought Dick Richardson interesting; here in my own flat I was beginning to think him impressive.

We did the washing-up together and after I had hung up the tea towel and turned toward him, he put his arms around me and kissed me. *This time*, I thought, *I really mustn't get it wrong.* I had no desire to participate in one of those wrestling, grappling scenes involving lots of insistence on the one hand and protesting refusals on the other, so I drew breath, and although it was a very nice kiss, I said firmly, "I know what we ought to do."

"Yes, so do I," he replied brazenly.

"We ought to go for a walk. Look, the rain has stopped."

He looked blankly at me and for a tiny moment I thought I *had* got it wrong. Then he burst out laughing, his curling bottom lip stretched beneath his beard. The threadbare duffle coat went on again. Then with some degree of tenderness he turned up my collar and tied my scarf around my neck.

We walked down toward the seafront and along the promenade

until we came to the rock garden. He took my hand and we walked in companionable silence. After a while he said, "Perhaps we should just be friends." And he smiled at me and put his arm round my shoulder. As he was about six foot, I felt as if I was being tucked under his arm. It gave me a feeling of immense security. I knew this was not just a trivial thing, but that I'd caught hold of something worth having.

CHAPTER 19

The Family

We continued to see each other on my days off, and despite his suggestion that perhaps we should just be friends he never stopped trying to seduce me. It was very difficult holding him at arm's length as I was absolutely dazzled by him. I thought everything he said was extraordinary. His comments and views seemed so incisive. I had never met anyone like him before.

He was going home to his family for Christmas and I to my mother, but one evening just before he left Portsmouth he invited me to go to the HMS Collingwood New Year Ball. I was delighted, particularly as naval dos were always wonderfully organized in those days and often amazingly glamorous. They are much less so nowadays: the "cuts" have put paid to that! Thanks to my father's unexpected Christmas gift of £10, I had enough money to buy a much coveted Laura Ashley dress. It was black and white check with a deep flounce in contrasting but complementary black and white polka dot. Di admired the style but thought it looked like a tablecloth. I loved it.

The day before the ball Dick called again, to say he would pick me up in a taxi. Anthea Seal handed me the phone with a resigned but wry expression. "You've got to tell him not to ring the ward."

"I have told him, but it's the only way he can contact me. I'll be quick."

I had just rung off when a thought occurred to me: much as I relished his company I wasn't sure I wanted to spend several hours dancing with someone who had two left feet. Pleasure in a dancing partner does rather suppose a certain prowess in stepping the light fantastic.

In the taxi on New Year's Eve I addressed the issue. "Can you ballroom dance?" I demanded, probably rather imperiously.

There was a slight pause and he looked startled, then the ironic smile that I was beginning to recognize so well appeared. "There is no such verb as 'to ballroom dance'," he replied gravely. I was to become very familiar with this sort of sardonic riposte. Then he grinned, "You'll have to wait and see, won't you!"

Actually I discovered he was a lovely dancer and particularly good at rock and roll. Like so many big men, he was light on his feet, with excellent rhythm. It was a wonderfully happy evening.

When midnight struck and kissing became widespread, I saw him looking for me across the bar, as we had been separated for the previous dance. His kiss was light but the embrace was close and his face was warm. "Happy New Year, Tiny," he said. It was the first time he used the name that he was to call me from then on and I was so happy I could only cling to his arms. I wished that he would say to me what I longed to say to him: that I was mesmerized by him, that I had never met anyone like him before, that I wanted to spend every minute of every day with him, and please, please, please would he love me back?

A week or so later he phoned me at the hospital again, either oblivious or indifferent to my telling him about the general rule about staff not receiving personal calls. Would I like to come home with him for the weekend? His brother Ed and wife Annie would be there and his sister too. It felt like a milestone in our relationship.

His parents, Ron and Eveline, lived in a pleasant 1930s chalet bungalow on the outskirts of Fleet. The house was warm and comfortable, pleasantly and elegantly furnished. His mother, a plump, quiet, pretty woman with dark hair, seemed a little shy. His father was grey-haired with intensely blue eyes, a tall, very good-looking man in his sixties, with something of Cary Grant about him. He was not in the least shy, and addressed me jovially as "young lady". They were both charming and welcoming.

All the family were there. I was a little overwhelmed at first, mainly because they were all so tall. Ron and Ed were both six foot plus and Dick only a little shorter. Lizzie their sister was five foot eleven in her stockinged feet and Annie, Ed's wife, towered above me. Eveline herself was probably, by my estimation, five foot seven. I felt a dwarf and rather at a disadvantage. I was quite pleased when everybody sat down.

I then made an astonishing discovery. Dick, my Dick, wasn't Dick at all. I thought I had misheard when his mother called him John.

"I thought you were called Dick," I said rather accusingly, feeling more than a bit foolish.

"I *am* called Dick, but my name is John. Ed's called Dick too, but as you know, his name is Edward."

"How odd! What's that all about?"

"Well, I think it's a service habit; you know, Chalky White, Dusty Miller, Dickie Byrd, Nobby Clarke."

"It was very difficult if both the boys were at home," his mother interjected.

"A girl might ring and ask for Dick. 'Which one?' I'd say. Both the boys were in the navy, both at HMS Collingwood, both with beards, both with glasses. Poor girls. I was always rather surprised that they persisted; eventually they would say something that distinguished one boy from the other. 'Ah,' I'd say, 'you're talking about the one that plays rugby! That'll be Ed.'"

So I had to learn to call him John. My brother and many of his naval friends continued to call him Dick for some time but eventually stopped, and he became John to everyone.

I knew I had fallen in love with John aka Dick, and by the end of that extraordinary weekend I was definitely in love with his parents too. It was two days of great happiness and discovery. Compared to my own somewhat dysfunctional family, this one seemed to me almost idyllic. Ron and Eveline's marriage appeared to incorporate a warm stability, an all-encompassing, reassuring quality. Most of all, this relationship was defined by their obviously deep love for each other and, by extension, their affection for their children and those to whom their children were attached.

Their kindness and civility were beguiling. Their house, John told me, and later I would discover, was regularly filled with family, including second cousins, and with other intimate and cherished company. They had friendships that extended back for decades, from their courtship and even from their early youth. For both of them hospitality seemed natural, welcomed and enjoyed. They adored being surrounded by intimates. This practice had filtered down to the second generation; John too had friendships he had nurtured since primary school. My own parents seemed to have lost touch with everybody, so their own world got smaller and smaller as they aged. They never seemed to hang on to friends. My father, twelve years younger than his sister, was estranged from her and had no contact with nephews and nieces, and although my mother was deeply attached to both her brothers, they lived some distance away and interaction was infrequent. They had an excuse; service life is not conducive to the maintenance of relationships.

However, despite all this human warmth, I was startled and amused, if rather taken aback, by the Richardsons' display of immense self-assurance, and I could see that this would be challenging. I had never met people whose belief in the probity of their personal values was so firm; each one had great certainty about their own standards. I never heard them condemn those of others and they weren't in the least patronizing or arrogant, but there was a very strong sentiment that they'd got it right.

I soon discovered that Ron and Eveline had similarly strong views on behaviour and morality. They weren't stuffy, but they were conservative and deeply disapproving of sexual misbehaviour, even of minor peccadilloes. Sometimes this made them rather inflexible. When Eveline's bridesmaid, I learned, began an affair with a Canadian during the war, she was banned from the house. She was a close friend, and John's godmother, so this was a harsh measure. Eveline met her on neutral ground – they still cared for her and valued her – but it would have been unthinkable to invite her and her partner into their home, so their front door was closed to her.

When the Canadian left at the end of the war she was welcomed back and readmitted. It says a great deal for her that she not only accepted the restrictions placed on her, but was cheerful about being welcomed back into the bosom of the family. She showed no resentment; clearly she respected their views.

Neither Ron nor Eveline came from a wealthy background and they had had to make considerable sacrifices when bringing up the children. Family holidays were simple, camping or caravanning, sometimes with friends, and even when Ron took up gliding it was as part of a syndicate and pretty much done on the cheap. All these admirable qualities of loyalty, fidelity, honesty, frugality, kindness, civility and moral rectitude were entrenched and passed down to their children, who were free to adopt them, adjust them or reject them. John took on board many of them, and as far as I know was not openly reproached for those he chose to ignore, though I was to learn this distressed his mother. His calm but firm declaration that he was an atheist she found hard to accept. She would have preferred him to say he was an agnostic, thinking I imagine that this was the lesser of the two evils, but this he thought dishonest. As an adolescent he had had vehement arguments with her, but as he grew up he saw how much it hurt her and so avoided contentious discussions. He seemed, however, to have no problem with dating an ex-nun!

CHAPTER 20

Weddings

In Portsmouth there were changes. Shortly before I met John, Di had met Peter, a naval officer, and it was the beginning of a serious relationship. He went to sea and they became engaged before he left. More significantly, on his return they bought a house, which they decided to move into. Di didn't want to pay a mortgage and rent for the flat, which I could see was sensible, although I felt some consternation. She had been my support since I had met her, four months after leaving my convent in Liverpool. Her advice, whether I asked for it or not, had been practical and usually very helpful. I had been welcomed into her family with great generosity and she felt like *my* family, so her departure left me in a quandary. I was hesitant about what to do. I didn't want to take another flatmate and didn't get on particularly well with the remaining one. It was a time of rather anxious uncertainty.

I don't know how long John took to think about it or indeed how long he had been thinking about it, but one evening in The Blackies he said, "Why don't you move in with me?"

Although I said yes, I knew this was far from ideal. The inhibitions I felt about this decision were underpinned by several things. His house was in a very pleasant suburb in the north of the city, but he had two tenants and I wasn't sure I wanted to be viewed as another tenant, albeit one with fringe benefits. Di was moving into a house with Peter, but *they* were going to get married, so respectability was maintained. My situation was ambiguous, as demonstrated very clearly by our landlady, who gave Di a small intimate gift as a wedding present and me a warm kiss on the cheek. Knowing that we were both ultimately departing, to our surprise and relief our landlords adopted Jeremy cat. "We might just as well," they said. "He clearly feels he belongs here."

We were both sorry to leave the flat, but looked forward to this change in our circumstances – Di, I have to say, with more confidence than me. John had not committed himself and although I would have married him had he asked me, he hadn't. I did feel I was burning my bridges when I took him up on his offer.

The other and subtler reservation about the wisdom of moving in with John was the need to ignore the curiously disapproving attitude of my colleagues at work.

There was a widely accepted myth about nurses. Like the theatrical masks representing comedy on one face and tragedy on the reverse, nurses were regarded either as angels or harlots. They were admired as reincarnations of "the lady with the lamp" by some, or viewed as "an easy lay" by others. In the seventies many nurses opted for dissimilation. If they were in a relationship, or even just cheerfully promiscuous, they hid it. Those who didn't were viewed with disapproval, because their behaviour called into question everybody else's.

All the old clichés about men not wanting "shop-soiled goods" or "not respecting a girl once they'd had their wicked way" were trotted out. Dire consequences were hinted at, and these often from women who were themselves sexually involved with their boyfriends. I remember a particularly pretty and vivacious girl who talked, with what was regarded as bare-faced boldness, about her colourful love life. "She'll never get a husband," was the received wisdom. She was one of the first in my group to get married. He was a rich farmer; they moved to his lovely house in Ireland where she lived in considerable comfort, producing four beautiful children.

So it was with some apprehension that I moved into John's large, if rather shabby, house. His parents, who naïvely hoped my bedroom would be my own, were dismayed when they realized the situation. My father, whose own life after leaving my mother had been very irregular, was furious, and made dramatic and ridiculous statements about wanting to meet John "sword in hand". My mother was unhappy, but sensibly said nothing and met John with equanimity if not with enthusiasm.

We continued to visit Ron and Eveline. I was certainly not barred from the house and continued to be welcomed with their usual charm and pleasure, although on one memorable occasion Eveline's organizational skills were sorely tested. Ed and Annie and Lizzie and her boyfriend also arrived. There were only two spare bedrooms and we were three extra couples. When John and I stayed we were naturally put in separate bedrooms, but what to do with six visitors, only two of whom were married? Her solution was practical and rather resourceful: all the men slept in one room and all the women in another. Ed protested on the grounds of his married status, but was overruled. At the end of the usual lovely, lively evening when we retired to bed, we made a joke of it all, lining up in our night clothes with candles in our hands. Our attended men were invited into the sitting room to kiss us chastely goodnight before retiring to our respective "dormitories". Eveline and Ron stood smiling benignly at us all. They really were the most delightful people.

We went for tea there one afternoon. John told me later about the following exchange. In the garden, Ron took him aside. "That little girl," he said, "seems to be very much in love with you. Don't you think you ought to do something about it?"

"Yes," was John's rather non-committal response. "I am thinking about it."

That evening back in Portsmouth he turned to me and said quietly, "Shall we get married then?"

It was so unexpected, I was taken aback and frankly a little sceptical. My response was unorthodox. Rather than casting myself into his arms and crying, "Yes, oh yes!" as I would have done a month or so before, I said cautiously, "When?" I had lived with this complex and unusual man for some weeks and had become used to his sometimes lateral thought processes and his irony.

He laughed aloud. "Tiny," he said, "you can say yes or you can say no; you really can't say when."

"OK. Yes, of course I'll marry you, but when?"

Without hesitation he replied, "November."

"November! Why November?"

"Di gets married in August. You don't want to upstage her, do you?"

We phoned his parents straight away. They were delighted but puzzled.

"Why didn't you tell us this afternoon?"

"We didn't know this afternoon! It's only just happened."

A few days later, in The Lanes in Brighton, we found a lovely Victorian ring, set with diamonds and sapphires. It was a little large, but I insisted on wearing it, saying I would get a jeweller to adjust it. I wanted to show it to my mother and Peter and Linda, whom we had arranged to meet that evening. My mother was ready to be offended when I foolishly revealed I had told my father first about our engagement.

"Mummy, you don't have a telephone and I knew I was seeing you before him. He hasn't seen the ring, for goodness' sake." I placated her but foresaw problems ahead for the wedding.

I was deliriously happy, even though I knew that some people initially, probably including Di, saw us as an ill-matched pair. Temperamentally we were very different. John was generally a quiet man, although when roused to anger could be very loud indeed. He was analytical, even introspective: all his actions were considered, and he was very confident of his judgment, which was usually acute. He enjoyed company, but was happier with a small group of friends than with a large assembly of acquaintances. His intellect was very powerful; I had never met anyone so well read in almost every field. He had an avid curiosity and the breadth of his knowledge was astonishing. His view of the world was often cynical, but he was a loyal, caring and generous friend.

I, on the other hand, was almost everything he was not: bouncy, impulsive, gregarious and spontaneous. Acting rashly without considering the consequences was a character defect of mine and often caused me, and inevitably others, pain. I could also be very, some might say, aggressively self-opinionated, and my judgment was sometimes questionable. But by nature I was affectionate, happy and trusting, and always expected and hoped for the best in people and situations.

I loved surprises; John loathed them. I hoped that we would complement each other and I think in the main we did. There were things we did have in common: we shared a sense of humour and a relative indifference to appearance and material things. John, like all his family, was a terrible hoarder – not because the things he clung to were intrinsically valuable but because they might "come in handy" and because he couldn't bear to throw away anything still working, even if its use was considerably circumscribed by its defects. I teased him, saying that I was sure he had somewhere a tin labelled "pieces of string too short to be of any use". We had vehement arguments about what I thought was the pointless storing of out-of-date and defective equipment. But he did acknowledge that my indifference to threadbare carpets and second-hand furniture was admirable.

Above all he was a protector, a caring man who showed his love in the way he cherished me. He found it difficult to express his feelings, whereas I was all verbal expression. We were both of us very tactile; he was particularly cuddly and I loved being cuddled.

At the hospital, with a ring on my finger, I too was now respectable. It was amazing what a difference a gold band with a few stones in it made!

Di's August wedding was getting ever closer. She asked Dee and me to be bridesmaids and we accepted with great pleasure. It was a busy time. I volunteered to make the bridesmaids' dresses and Di accepted. Her mother was horrified at the thought of "home-made dresses"! But when they were finished she thought them delightful and I was so pleased to do it for Di, who had been such a good friend to me. It was a beautiful sunny day. Di and Peter made a handsome couple and she looked very happy.

Then I had time to think about our own celebration, and began in a very simple way to make some preparation for it. We decided on as quiet a wedding as we could get away with. We would have to fund it ourselves. Neither of my parents had the resources for the big white wedding, even had I wanted it, and John's temperament meant that he had a horror of the sort of occasion where he would be the centre of attention and have to make a speech. He had suffered, and was to continue suffering, from periods of acute anxiety associated with depression. I don't know if it was the impending wedding that brought it on but he was manifestly unwell around that time, which was a further reason for having a low-key affair. The family were invited as a matter of course. We agreed that we would include John's godmother, mainly because John thought she would be very hurt not to come, and I insisted on Di. Actually, I knew there were more than one or two on my side who would be hurt not to receive an invitation. Di's parents, who had been so good to me, might justifiably feel a bit put out, and sweet Dee who had shared so many moments. I felt sorry about not having her.

Despite his atheism John recognized my needs, respected my faith and agreed to be married in church. In the seventies there were very few places licensed for weddings; it was church or register office, and he felt the latter was a bit "flat". I made an appointment to see the parish curate, a gentle Irishman called Father Toumey. I had some concerns, as I knew that "mixed marriages", a Catholic marrying a non-Catholic, were sometimes problematic. The non-Catholic partner had to promise to "bring up any children born of the union, in the Catholic faith". I rather wondered what John would make of that. I warned him about it but he just smiled and looked a little quizzical. In the event his handling of the situation was masterly.

"I'm not sure I can promise to do that," he said gravely.

Poor Father Toumey blushed and began to sweat; he was twisting his fingers together in some anxiety. "Well," he replied, clearing his throat, "is there any way we could reach some sort of compromise? I hope, for example, you wouldn't oppose your wife if *she* wanted to bring the children up as Catholics?"

"No, I wouldn't oppose her at all. But I rather hope she will eventually begin to think as I do; that is, as an atheist."

The poor man gave a gasp of horror and rolled his eyes toward me.

I soothed him calmly. "Please, Father, don't bother; don't be alarmed, there's no chance of that, none whatsoever. I'm an ex-nun."

John reassured him too. "Relax, Father; I'm agreeing to be married in your church. I'm hardly likely to browbeat my wife about her faith. This I will commit to. I will do my very best to bring up any children as good citizens, with a decent moral code of conduct. And I will not oppose their faith if they have one."

He seemed to be happy with that. We agreed a date, 10 November, and that was that.

"You were unkind to tease him, poor man," I said reproachfully in the car on the way home.

John looked startled. "I wasn't teasing him. I meant it!"

"What, about trying to convert me to atheism?"

"Yes, of course, but only if you show any interest in it." He laughed.

I think he quite enjoyed outraging people or startling them. When he first told colleagues about getting married, he would ask them if they wanted to see a photo of his fiancée. They were polite enough to say yes, although they must have been surprised: this was not John Richardson's style at all. He would then solemnly produce a photo of me as a nun in the religious habit – long black dress, white bonnet and veil – and wait, poker-faced, for the reaction. "It was such good value," he said. "People just didn't know what to say."

He began to take me to visit some of his oldest and closest friends, people with whom he'd been to school or university, or the one or two intimates he'd made in the navy. We stayed with several over quite a short period. I had the feeling I was being shown to them for their approval, although they were all delightful. I hope they did approve; I certainly approved of them.

I hit a serious snag with my mother. My brother and Linda had no advice to offer me about her. She was ruthless in her refusal to share any part of the day, *my day*, with my father. If he was to be there she wouldn't come. He was almost as bad, saying he didn't think it a good idea for him to attend either. They just couldn't face meeting each other; he, I suspect, from shame and she from fury. The suggested compromise, that she, as a practising Catholic, should come to the church and he come to our very modest reception, was met with such an expression of outrage on her part that it seemed pointless to insist. My father said he'd pay for the champagne, which he did, but he confessed to me later that he had spent a very sad day on 10 November. My mother came to the wedding, both to the church and to the lunch. "Reception" seems too grand a word for our pleasant buffet afterwards.

At IBM John had a colleague who, with his wife, had a sideline catering for small events and we booked them and asked them to make a wedding cake. It all seemed so easy and unstressed. They were pleasant people to deal with and seemed to think a wedding party of twelve people was no problem at all.

I wasn't very sure what to wear and thought again that I might find something romantic in Laura Ashley. I didn't hold up much hope of finding anything in Portsmouth, which in the seventies was still a pretty down-at-heel city, so went to Brighton. I was not looking for the "big meringue" or even a white dress at all, but by chance, and just when I had started to despair of finding anything, saw a wedding dress that I thought quite lovely in a bridal shop. It was a narrow, sleeveless empire line dress, with a round neck edged with scalloped lace and matched with a beautiful hooded coat with a little train. It was creamy white and fitted perfectly, even to the length, which was always a problem for someone as short as I am.

It was in the sale and I bought it straight away. Having ultimately chosen white, I wanted something a little different to offset the whole thing. I ordered a bouquet from a local florist. She was astonished by my choice and tried hard to persuade me to have roses and freesias, but I was adamant. I chose daisy chrysanthemums in a lovely shade of amber and found shoes to match. Later, when some French friends saw the photos, they expressed something approaching dismay. In France, chrysanthemums are uniquely associated with death! I thought it gave a charming autumnal touch to the outfit.

On 9 November I slipped along to the church and went to confession. I left John to wait for me in the pub opposite. When my sad little stories were over and I had expressed contrition for all of them, including what one might call my "present irregular situation", the priest (not the pleasant young Irishman but the other, rather tough, old parish priest) said, "Let's see. Is there anything we can do about your current situation?"

He sounded so depressed that I was delighted to reply, "Yes, Father. Actually, we're getting married tomorrow, here in St Coleman's."

His voice brightened noticeably. "Isn't that just grand! You'll say a decade of the rosary and thank the Blessed Virgin for bringing you home to us!"

I was very moved at the kind response and thought of the unpleasant priest I'd met in Poole, with his savage indictment of my sinfulness and God's punishment.

"Well?" said John. "Are you cleansed?" He grinned but had a glass of wine waiting for me. "After all that guilt and anguish you could probably do with this."

"It is rather cathartic – confession, I mean. But tonight, if you don't mind, we'll sleep in separate rooms. Will you humour me in this?"

And he did.

The weather on the 10th was as vile as it could be. What can one expect if one chooses to marry in November? The rain was pitiless and so unrelenting that the photographer took all the photos inside the church. I couldn't have cared less. It all went beautifully. The French say "*mariage pluvieux, mariage heureux*" (rainy wedding, happy marriage). As my mother and I were the only two Roman Catholics I didn't subject the rest to a nuptial mass; the wedding service was simple and appropriate.

Our caterers were excellent and it was all very loving and happy and rather jolly. There were no speeches, so we were spared the usual embarrassment often associated with these occasions. We drank my father's champagne and ate salmon and roast beef with potato salad and coleslaw. It was not very adventurous but we also had avocado and asparagus; the first time I had ever tasted them. By 5:30 p.m. it was all over and the last of the guests had gone. I took off my wedding dress and changed into slacks and a jumper, and John changed out of his suit into something casual. Then we went down into town to Kings Theatre to see *Godspell*. In the foyer we bumped into a colleague from St Mary's.

"Eleanor!" she said. "What on earth are you doing here? I thought you were getting married today."

"We did," I said, laughing delightedly. "We did!"

PART 4

Marriage and Motherhood: 1973–79

CHAPTER 21

Further Adaptation

At about 10 a.m., the day after we were married, there was a ring at the door. I found Peter and Linda outside. They had noticed, they said, that there was a considerable amount of poached salmon left over; would we like some help with polishing it off? We could only laugh at their nerve.

We were still in our dressing gowns, but invited them in and we all had brunch together, which included not only the salmon but the beef and what was left of all the salads. John discovered an unopened bottle of champagne in the fridge, obviously overlooked, and we drank Buck's Fizz and ate wedding cake. We didn't get rid of Peter and Linda till about 2 p.m., when John and I left for Oxford to see my father.

We stayed at the Eastgate Hotel in the High Street and had an indifferent meal with him, but I felt I owed him some sign of appreciation for the champagne. He seemed relatively relaxed about having been sidelined and expressed some relief that he had avoided what he was sure would have been awkward for everybody. I thought both my parents terribly selfish, but I knew their separation had been bitter. I accepted my brother's view that it had been a hard one to call, and that their presence would have caused general unease. In such a small gathering, their mutual antagonism would have dominated the event.

At the hospital on Tuesday, when I returned to work, astonishment was expressed not only that we had had no honeymoon but that there was no plan for a delayed one. John's houses in Carmarthen Avenue and his job with "Big Blue" put him in the category of a rather well-off young man. So the general feeling was that either he was parsimonious (look at the skimpy wedding!) or he was eccentric. I favoured the latter. "Don't you mind?" I was asked repeatedly. The honeymoon, one recently married nurse told me, was essential to recover from the exhausting activity of the months before the wedding! "I never moved from the poolside," she told me. "I was utterly drained." My reply that we hadn't had any frenetic activity as ours had been a really low-key affair didn't seem to cut the mustard. I was irritated to see pity on her face. I was disappointed that so many people attached so much importance to the outward display and saw a modest low-key event as a paltry hole-in-the-corner affair. It occurred to me that perhaps they thought I was pregnant.

I settled down very happily into married life. It didn't make very much difference on a day-to-day basis from our previous life together. We went to work, came home, had supper, read or watched TV. Neither of us had any inclination to do any interior decoration, although the house, a comfortable 1930s semi, was badly in need of it. The large garden, which at one point had been prettily landscaped with terracing and some quite exotic flowering shrubs, had become a wilderness. We ignored the resulting jungle cheerfully, enjoying it when it was sunny and warm, and occasionally taking secateurs or even a saw to the undergrowth when it threatened to encroach too closely on the house or hinder our progress to the end of the lawn.

By the time we were married there only remained one lodger in our house, and she was a pleasant, affable girl who enjoyed living with us and was no bother at all. This was another situation that seemed to cause bemusement among my colleagues. Their comments, which they didn't hesitate to make, ranged from the almost insolent "How odd. How long is she going to stay?" or "Don't you find it a constraint; I mean not being private?" to the tentative "Is she a family friend?" or "Have you known her long?"

I was beginning to accept that our married setup was not in the ordinary way of things. Perhaps, I thought, some suspected, or may even have pruriently hoped, that we were involved in a ménage à trois. After a while it all settled down, and the curiosity diminished as other events superimposed themselves. John, if he was free, picked me up from work, and was seen, by those who crossed his path, to be a perfectly pleasant man despite the black beard and the minimal wedding. Those who came to know him, like Di, began to like him. Never one to hang on to an unjustified suspicion, she saw that I was happy and acknowledged that maybe he was, after all, the man for me.

We had sparky moments though, he and I, that stemmed both from our different temperaments and from his tendency to suppress his irritation until, unable to contain it, there was an outburst.

One evening, tired after a long week and looking forward to a lie in, he expressed with some vehemence his irritation when I asked for a lift into work. I was on duty over the weekend and the local bus service on Saturday and Sunday was erratic.

"Tiny, I really wish you would pass your driving test. You must see that I don't relish the thought of having to drive you around for the rest of your natural. Ed has got a Morris 1000 of mine that you can *have* as your own, once you pass the test!"

I can't say that the promise of a car was the motivating force but finally, on the fourth attempt, I passed. I arrived home with the precious piece of paper. John was in the kitchen. "At last!" he said, then came to hug me.

"I want to shout, like Mr Toad, 'The open road, the dusty highway… Travel, change, interest, excitement!… the ever-changing horizons.' How free I feel!"

"You do realize," replied my ever literal husband, "that the pieces you have quoted, or rather misquoted, applied to Toad's pleasure in his *caravan* not the car, and," he went on, "Toad's adventures in his motor were unfortunate. He ended up in prison, having written off the car, if my memory is correct."

Prophetic words: within six months I had reversed into a telegraph post, scraped the shabby old Morris along the offside of a smart little Ford in mint condition (because I had drawn up too close to it in an attempt to reverse my old banger into a parking space) and then dented both wings in separate incidents in a multi-storey car park.

"Remember I told you when you first got your licence that in this day and age people have incidents in their cars all the time – with all the traffic on the road it's inevitable – and how you weren't to be scared to tell me, or think I'd be furious?" John's voice was very calm. "You've had four shunts in six months and I really think that's quite enough."

It was the first time I'd seen him angry and it shook me a little. I'd like to say I mended my ways, but there have been, in the course of our life together, several other accidents. Thankfully none of them were serious as far as driver or passengers were concerned, although some of the cars were irreparable. John wrote off a dear little MG Midget and once, coming home from the airport after a long-haul flight, he rammed a taxi as we drove round the Devil's Punch Bowl near Guildford. He had been driving since he was sixteen and his experience on the road certainly gave him the edge on me. I didn't concentrate enough, wanted to chat and look at the countryside; he drove too fast and took risks.

There were other areas of contention. John had grown up in a home where both his parents were frugal and husbanded their resources. He was used to a certain discipline in budgeting and expenditure. Temperamentally I was casual and even careless, and this was not helped by eight years in a convent. During that time I had had no dealings with money. All my needs were provided for, even the most basic. I wanted for nothing.

I never knew the cost of heating or lighting any of the large convents that I had lived in, nor the size of the bills for the water and sewerage. I didn't ask, and the community was never told. I had never paid a bill in my life. Even when I left the community, I had, thanks to Di, been protected. She was a great organizer and dealt with almost all the day-to-day material problems. If she said my share of the bill was x amount, I gave her cash or wrote a cheque, once I'd learned how to do so. I was complicit in this way of life, only too happy for someone else to do things for me, but it meant that budgeting for a household was a whole new skill, and one that I was very slow to learn. John was completely bemused by my inability to live within the planned expenditure. I began to feel very inadequate and, even worse, ashamed, but these two sentiments didn't help me at all. My financial contribution as a midwife was not insignificant but still far less than John's and I knew he was often irritated by what he saw as my fecklessness.

If I'd had any sense I'd have gone to Eveline, my mother-in-law, and asked her to advise me, but I never thought of it and I imagine she never thought that I needed that sort of help. I had married a man, as they say, of property, who already owned his house and was paying the mortgage. He never suggested I contribute to it or take over the responsibility for paying the household bills. I was, in the words of Willie Hamilton about some member of the Royal Family, "an expensive kept woman".

I was nevertheless very anxious to be a good wife and to make John comfortable at home, although housework was never very high on my agenda. I had done a surfeit of it as a nun. It took a long time for me to get even a modicum of sensible organization. In marrying him, I had also been drawn into participating, sharing and indeed benefiting from his property portfolio. The bookkeeping associated with this, in those pre-computer days, was very time-consuming. It was not an activity that I would have voluntarily undertaken, and I didn't enjoy it. I also undertook to deal on a personal level with the tenants: to collect the rents, to change light bulbs, to unblock the sinks when they were too indifferent or idle to do it themselves. But it was always a chore, and I felt guilty because I knew that most of the burden fell on my husband and that I didn't do my share either well or particularly willingly and yet benefited from the lifestyle it provided.

Later we had a sharp exchange because I refused to apply for an administrative post on the maternity unit. This job came about because of the restructuring of the midwifery service. I felt I was seriously under-qualified for it and above all it would considerably reduce my contact hours on the ward. John's argument was that if I got the job I could negotiate more contact hours on the strength of needing to keep my hand in. The real clincher was that it was better paid.

"I don't care if it's better paid," I said vehemently. "I didn't become a midwife to sit in an office drowning in paperwork!"

"You wouldn't talk like that if you were a man," he replied bitterly, and there was considerable coolness for a few days. Again I felt as if I was failing him.

Cooking, on the other hand, was something I really enjoyed and became good at. The first year we were married, the family came to us for Christmas. The turkey was enormous. I had over-catered and it barely fitted into the oven, but overall the meal was a triumph. Eveline provided the Christmas pudding. I now, with unreserved pleasure, called her "Mum", though not in front of my mother, who was always a little touchy about it. The whole event was a great success and I felt this was something I could contribute.

John would have lived on bread and cheese or tinned mince, left to his own devices. Apart from loving me, something he found difficult to express in words, he actually enjoyed being married. He had found being a bachelor lonely. He relished the company and the intimacy of our life and I was excused many things because I was loving and cuddly, and by the same token I tolerated his obsessions.

Our social life expanded, both at the hospital and among John's naval friends. He now had somewhere he could entertain. I gave up smoking because he hated it and it was beginning to be frowned on generally, but we drank with pleasure. John had taken an interest in wine when in the navy and this continued, so at home or when friends came round, we drank some very good wine indeed. Parties, however, normally provided what a friend of mine called red or white "infuriator" and, particularly at hospital parties, discretion was not always the better part of valour.

We went to one given by a doctor and his wife, colleagues. John's mum and dad were staying with us, but we excused ourselves, as this invitation predated their visit. I finished work late after a hectic day and by the time I had changed and got to the place, it was about 9 p.m. The room, dimly lit with candles, was heaving. I found John in a corner nursing a pint of beer.

"I'll be with you in a minute," I said. "I must get a drink."

By the time I'd got back to him, I'd had several and was feeling relaxed and cheerful. The workload had been so busy that day that I hadn't had a lunch break, and apart from a biscuit with tea in the afternoon, had eaten nothing. It was barely 10 p.m. but I had been drinking since I arrived. My tiredness seemed to have evaporated! The next glass or two left me a little lightheaded and the one following that, blurry-eyed. My hostess arrived to announce food and placed a large bowl of baked potatoes on a table already laid with pâté, cheese and salad. The part of my mind that was still functioning thought, "I'll be fine once I've had some food."

Unthinkingly I picked up a baked potato; it was straight from the oven and piping hot. In shock, transferring it from one hand to another, I staggered back in the vague direction of a sofa, which in the dim light and through my alcoholic daze I had thought was vacant. When I felt the edge behind my legs, I sat down. It felt very lumpy and when I groped behind me to remove what I thought was a cushion, I discovered, to my embarrassed astonishment and no less hers, that I had sat down on the lap of a very surprised Indian lady anaesthetist.

I just about managed to mumble an apology and then with what I hoped was a winning smile took her hand and placed my baked potato into her palm. She dropped it instantly and stared at me. John appeared beside me.

"I need to go home," I said.

He guided me toward the door and I gave a vague wave in the direction of my hosts.

At home I heard John laughingly say to his mother, who had come to the door, "Can you give me a hand with Eleanor? She is rather the worse for wear."

Inside the house I was suddenly and violently sick. I looked with horror and shame at the purple puddle, obviously red "infuriator".

"You poor little thing!" My mother-in-law's voice was thick with indignation and sympathy. "Somebody's been giving you some perfectly horrid, rough old wine!"

Oh yes, I had definitely chosen well when I picked the Richardsons.

CHAPTER 22

Honeymoon

In March 1974 we went to Australia for three weeks and so redeemed John's reputation at the hospital. On his mother's side there were family and friends in Sydney. Some had been in England during or just after the war and another distant cousin, known in the family as EP, came for the Queen's coronation and stayed for five years.

It was a wonderful holiday and an amazing experience. Such a young and sometimes brash country can be both exciting and challenging. It was hard to explain that although I thought everything delightful and the climate and ease of life very appealing, I really didn't want to leave Britain definitively. Many Australians believed then that life in Oz was just like life in England, but with better weather and a higher standard of living, and expressed astonishment that once we had seen what the country had to offer, we would not immediately set about applying for immigrant status. However, we found the sense of isolation daunting. John, an avid "news gatherer", fretted about the lack of international affairs in Australian newspapers.

In particular, while we were there, the British government granted security of tenure to tenants in furnished accommodation which, in our case, would mean that our property portfolio's value was seriously compromised. There was almost nothing about it in the Australian press. We felt we were a very long way from home. Today there is no problem – the internet, mobile phones and the internationalization of big business and financial institutions means there is an automatic blending of information, but in the seventies it was not the case. To us, Australia, for all its size and multinational population, seemed curiously parochial.

Certainly Sydney was sophisticated, and parts were architecturally interesting. Not unreasonably, anything over 150 years was considered very old. Aboriginal history and culture was, with rare exceptions, completely sidelined. Some of the nineteenth-century houses with their pretty filigree "iron lace" verandas were charming and very sought after. At the other extreme, some of the modern architecture was stunningly beautiful. The Opera House was such a statement of self-confidence it was impossible not to be impressed, whether one liked and admired it or not. We thought it magnificent.

Out in the country towns, the large, low bungalows were roomy and comfortable, although their corrugated-iron roofs seemed slightly incongruous. We learned that this type of roofing had a historical dimension and was considered a "feature", having been one of the oldest forms of building material in the early settlers' time. We found these townships, with their wide streets lined with mostly single-storey buildings, immensely interesting. Each had a fascinating timeline and more often than not a name that to our ears was not only exotic but strangely evocative: Come by Chance, Broken Hill, Jimcumbilly. Others harked back to the old country. We lost count of the times we saw familiar names: Balmoral, Braemar, Dunoon (my own birthplace), even Newcastle.

We stayed in Sydney with EP. Her proper name was Eleanor Mary Platt and in her own family she was known as Aunty Mary. She was a solicitor and worked in the business centre. She had started her working life as a bookkeeper. When her boss, the head of the firm, realized that his son, whom he had intended to take on as a partner, was not able to pass his law exams, EP was asked to study law herself. All her fees would be met on the proviso that she worked for the firm once qualified, which she did.

Later she also became an accountant and was at one time, so I was told, the most highly qualified professional woman in New South Wales. She was unmarried and rather masculine in appearance, with very short brown hair. Dressed for work she was the very epitome of the businesswoman: neat grey suit, white blouse buttoned to the neck, stockings, court shoes and gloves. At home she wore trousers and tee-shirts, or a jumper if it was cool. I never saw make-up on her face. Her 1920-ish house was in Cremorne, a pleasant leafy suburb with good shops and restaurants. Her welcome was very warm and she hugged John with evident affection, calling him "Jonathan", which she seemed to think was the full version of his name. We were rather jet lagged, so I didn't at first notice the oddness of her behaviour toward me.

After three or four days I said to John, "She's not talking to me."

"What do you mean, she's not talking to you? I've heard her talking to you. She's just asked what we've done today."

"No, she asked *you* what we've done today. She's just asked *you* what you'd like for supper and when I said we were thinking of going to the zoo tomorrow, she told *you* the things we might be particularly interested in seeing and the best way to get there."

John thought about it and had to agree. "Yes, you're right. What do you want me to do?"

"Nothing. She'll probably get over it. I think it's a jealousy thing. You were her special little boy in London and she wants me to know it. She doesn't want to share you. Remember the look on her face when she saw we had pushed the single beds together?"

It had been a pretty pointless exercise actually, as one bed was a good three inches higher than the other, but we felt closer.

Dear EP, she did get over it, and we became good friends by the end of the holiday. She had an affectionate nature and a warm heart, but her spinster status tended to make her very possessive. She was once unwise enough to say about John, "After all, I've known him longer than you."

I felt a deep flash of anger but managed to say with a smile, "Yes, you have; you are very lucky. I'm doing my best to make up for lost time and we know different things about him, don't we?"

She had a sixteen-year-old niece, Sue, who was at Pymble Ladies' College in Sydney, whom we met briefly at EP's home. Years later when Sue was married, this jealousy scenario was repeated. EP did not like to share those she loved.

"She was vile to Mark," Sue told me with a laugh, "just horrible, but she got over it. They are good friends now."

During our trip, we went up country to visit Sue's parents, EP's brother and sister-in-law, Ted and Lucie. They lived in Dubbo, about four or five hours north-west of Sydney – in those days a town of some 25,000 people and a big agricultural centre. The facilities in the town were excellent; it was a clean, lively place with good shops, sports centres and restaurants. The countryside around was flat and arid, and it was suffocatingly hot! This, I thought, was the real Australia, where people lived close to the soil and had an intimate connection with nature. The farms or properties in the area were vast, thousands of acres, and the flocks of sheep were enormous – 20–30,000. I found it incredible that people could raise stock here. Compared to England's lush pasture, it looked poor grazing! In Sydney, we could have been in any dazzling urban centre, but here I felt we were in the real outback, although I was corrected about that.

"Nah, the outback's in the middle. Here we are out in the bush a bit, but the town's just fine. We've got all we need. We even get the opera and the ballet here... for those who like that sort of thing!"

The friendliness that Ted and Lucie showed us was irresistible. They had a party and invited friends that EP knew; they also invited a younger couple of about our age. "So you don't have to chat to old boilers like us," said Lucie cheerfully.

The young couple were good fun and had obviously come to enjoy themselves. When we said how much we loved Australia, we were immediately asked, yet again, when we were moving out there! They were keen to show off just a little, and produced a case of sparkling wine called Blue Rhapsody, which was being marketed as "the fizz to match your jeans". I drank it happily, although it smelled of antifreeze and tasted like cough medicine.

"No thanks," said EP. "I prefer something out of a bottle with a label I recognize." She had a Johnnie Walker whisky.

It was just as well she had something to occupy her; one of the less attractive features of Australian life then, and particularly up country, was the extreme misogyny we noticed. Even in this delightful company, the men retired to the kitchen and left the women in the sitting room, where the conversation revolved around domestic issues or the various women's clubs. Every now and then the kitchen door would open, a head would appear and a voice call, "Do ya want a beer, John?" He kept saying "yes" in the hope someone would bring him one. Eventually he understood and joined the masculine society in the kitchen. EP, who had grown up on a farm, been treated by her father as a boy, slaughtering sheep by the time she was ten, and who probably knew more about live stock prices than any of them, or at least as much as, fell asleep before 10 p.m. from sheer boredom.

The holiday passed all too quickly and we were both back at work by April. It was cold and rainy and I missed the Australian sun, but the shabby warmth of our home was welcoming and Mum — my mother-in-law — had made us new curtains for the bedroom.

Chapter 23

Disaster

John and I laughed that we were now a respectable married couple, having eventually had a sort of belated honeymoon. We became surprisingly traditional, inviting people to dinner and throwing a couple of parties. I believe that the shabbiness of our interior decor, the unkempt state of the garden and the continued presence of a tenant was still a source of puzzlement to some.

In the autumn I went to Rome for several days with my mother. We had an excellent holiday. She had begun to go there regularly. Indeed, after her first trip, the year she moved to Brighton, she so fell in love with the city she never went anywhere else. As we shared a room, I soon realized that insomnia was still a problem for her, but she seemed to cope and her nocturnal restlessness didn't slow her up during the day. She was bright and happy and was wonderfully knowledgeable about the city, taking me not only to ancient and Catholic Rome, but to areas not usually frequented by tourists.

In the spring of 1975 John and I decided the time had come to think about having a family. We had discussed at some length the possible problems associated with my gynaecological history and that I might have difficulty conceiving because of the STD that I had contracted, so I was both astonished and delighted to fall pregnant very quickly. I missed a period and there were immediate physical changes that made it, I believed, a certainty. I was off duty after a spell of nights and John had days owed following a stretch of overtime. We planned to use the time to visit friends in Birmingham and Monmouth, so I decided to wait until our return before doing a pregnancy test.

The morning we were due to set off I had some cramps and a little spotting. In a panic I phoned my GP, who came out to the house and reassured me. His attitude was pragmatic. He told me to take some paracetamol; he saw no reason to delay going away. "Spotting is fairly common. If it's healthy, it will stick," he said. "If not, it's better you lose it early rather than later."

I thought this was harsh but I could see the sense in it. John was hesitant about going, but the weather was fine and I preferred not to sit at home worrying. Regular doses of paracetamol eased the abdominal discomfort and we set off. I felt rather better in Birmingham, but by the Saturday in Monmouth I was in a great deal of discomfort.

John decided that rather than returning home to Portsmouth, we should go straight to his parents' house in Fleet, where he could leave me with his mother. She would know what to do, he said, if I was miscarrying. I was beginning to feel so ill I was glad for all decisions to be taken out of my hands. We arrived around tea-time and I went straight to bed. I had begun to bleed a little, this time fresh blood. Their local GP came about 6 p.m. and examined me.

"I think we have to assume that you are miscarrying." He was rather cool and unsympathetic. I imagine he was irritated by being called out on a Sunday evening. He approved the paracetamol, saying only, "Two every four hours. No more, mind."

By 10 p.m. I was in such pain I could hardly speak, and my abdomen was swollen and tense. The GP was called again. This time he was considerably more alarmed and consequently more sympathetic. Just before the ambulance arrived, he gave me an injection of pethidine. I had eaten nothing, but had drunk two cups of tea since arriving at my in-laws' home. As the paramedics manoeuvred me downstairs on a sort of carrying chair, Mum going ahead to guide them, I was suddenly violently sick. "Sorry, Mum," I managed to say. "I mustn't make a habit of this."

In the hospital I was kept under observation for about an hour, and just before midnight I was taken to theatre. I was not suffering a miscarriage; I was suffering a life-threatening situation, an ectopic pregnancy.

When I woke properly the next morning, I was only aware of a generalized soreness. Everything seemed very bright and I shut my eyes against the glare. I explored my body cautiously, and found a dressing beneath my hospital gown. It caused some pain when I touched it. I was aware of someone or something beside the bed. It took an immense effort to turn my head and open my eyes; everything seemed to be moving unbearably slowly. A nurse shifted into my field of vision.

"I'm just changing your drip." She sounded bright and cheery. "This is the last unit of blood; later we'll put up a saline drip."

"How many units have I had?"

"Just three." She was moving away. I wanted her to stop; there were things I wanted to ask. My mouth felt dry, my tongue furred; the taste in my mouth was vile. I vaguely remembered being sick on the stairs in Mum's house.

"Can I have a drink?"

"I'll ask the doctor; he'll be around to see you in a moment."

I wondered hazily where John was. I wished he was with me.

"Your husband," she said, as if anticipating my question, "has gone home to get you some things – washing stuff and nighties. He'll be back soon."

The doctor who appeared at the end of my bed was kind but direct. "I'm afraid you had an ectopic pregnancy; you really lost quite a lot of blood. I am very sorry about the pregnancy, but you will be fine now."

I could only think of one thing and I could hear how tremulous my voice was. "Have you saved the tube? I only had one; please tell me that you saved it."

"I'm so sorry," he replied gently. "With this condition, the tube is just blown apart. There's nothing to save."

There's nothing to save. I thought that sounded pretty definitive. I felt overwhelmed with wretchedness, and looked wordlessly at him; then a terrible mixture of rage and grief welled up, mixing with the sour, acrid taste in my mouth. It caught at the back of my throat and burst out in an awful howl.

"Oh, God! I came out of a convent to marry and have children.

Please don't tell me it's all over."

John appeared like a shadow behind him, then came round to the side of the bed and took my hands. His own were very cold. He looked pale, tired and very distressed.

"Don't cry, Tiny; don't cry. It'll be fine. Truly, it'll be fine."

The rest of the day I drifted in and out of sleep. Every time I opened my eyes John was sitting beside me. He looked exhausted. In the evening, nurses came to wash me and sit me up, and at last I had a cup of tea. It tasted wonderful.

Over the next day or two I began to get up a little, stagger to the toilet and sit out of bed. Then on the fourth day I developed a breathing problem. Every indrawn breath was painful. On the plus side, I stopped agonizing about my loss as I was too busy worrying that I might have a clot on the lung and be facing sudden death. An X-ray revealed pleurisy; it eventually settled, but it left me weak and my recovery was slow.

In very general terms, when talking beforehand about having a family, we had spoken lightly and casually of adoption. John knew my history, so it had always been a vague, fall-back position. Now in hospital, having learned the disastrous outcome of my waywardness, it seemed vital to me that we move forward into this new dimension.

While in hospital, the hospital social worker came to see me. At my request she had contacted Hampshire Social Services' adoption department. The surgeon had written a letter to support our application. The papers applying for adoption, I was told, were on their way. It was all happening very fast.

In my pain, both physical and emotional, I had given little thought to John's position in all this. My actions, so often impetuous, ran true to form. I was the barren one. But he was also grief-stricken. He said later that he fully supported the idea of adoption; he would just have liked a little more time to get used to the idea. He had always imagined children of his own and he needed to think through the implications of not having natural children with me.

After ten days, I went to my in-laws' kind and friendly house to rest and be pampered. I sat in their comfortable sitting room, reading and listening to the radio. John returned to work, coming back to Fleet in the evening. It was a long day for him. Mum, who was also working, came home at lunchtime to check I was all right and to make me soup and chicken sandwiches. Eventually I began to feel better and daringly walked to the end of the road and back, a trek that exhausted me. Each day I improved, and after a fortnight we returned to Portsmouth.

I was off work for six weeks. I seriously considered giving up midwifery for general nursing, but on reflection thought it was a bad idea. Once trained, I had never practised as a general nurse. There would have been a loss of seniority and I was out of touch with new procedures. I went to see Matron Upman, who had first interviewed me at St Mary's, and asked if a post could be found for me in the antenatal and postnatal clinics. I was uncertain about how I would cope with delivering babies. Antenatal and postnatal clinics, while very important, are more detached from the hands-on activity on the wards. I also felt that the regular hours, 8:15 a.m. till 5 p.m., would fit in better with what I hoped would be the events associated with adoption.

She was extremely sympathetic and found a sister's slot for me in the maternity outpatients. So began a calmer time in my nursing life. The clinics were busy and not without their dramas, but I was home every night before 6 p.m. and left in the morning at 7:50 a.m. I didn't have to work at nights or at the weekend, and had all bank holidays off; it was wonderful. There was no overtime either, but I thought it was a price worth paying!

CHAPTER 24

Moving House

For some time before my ectopic pregnancy, John and I had been talking about moving house. It had become a frustrating experience – mainly because we had no very clear idea of what we were actually looking for. Once home and back at work, I was rather pleased to have something to take my mind off the recent traumatic events, particularly as we had heard nothing from the adoption department.

Ed and Annie entered into the spirit of our house-hunting and came up with suggestions for romantic, picturesque and totally impractical cottages in the depths of the countryside, most of which required an inordinate amount of work and several thousand pounds spent on them to make them habitable. John, with all his steady and rational thought processes, seemed, I was beginning to think, to be completely devoid of any aesthetic appreciation. He was very keen on an ugly little bungalow, admittedly on the edge of a charming and pretty village, that had a huge electricity pylon at the bottom of the garden. He was certain that we could get planning permission to add a second storey and it would then, he felt, be a fine family house with spectacular views.

My response was testy. "It's got a pylon at the bottom of the garden! What views are you talking about?" In the end I said I would infinitely prefer to remain in our warm, comfortable 1930s semi, which already had a bathroom, thank you very much, and central heating to boot. Given our mutual lack of enthusiasm for DIY, I really thought that the eighteenth-century cottage that Ed and Annie were so enthusiastic about, and which needed completely gutting, was a non-starter.

Then one evening my husband came home with a photo and details for a house about a mile away from our current home. It was a handsome, early nineteenth-century house. The Old Rectory was just within the city boundary and next door to a small Victorian neo-gothic church. It was well set back and shielded by yew trees, so was not visible from the road. It had been divided into two in about 1928 when it was no longer suitable as a vicarage, and the larger five-bedroom portion was for sale. Inside, it took our breath away. It had been built on strictly Palladian classical lines; the proportions of the rooms were so perfect that we didn't at first notice how large they were.

What we loved, and what amazed us most of all, was the circular hall that rose up through the first floor to a galleried landing lit by a glass lantern. We had never seen anything like this in a domestic house. As we were led from room to room by the delightful elderly owners, I grabbed John's arm and hissed, "We've got to have it!" The house was exquisitely furnished with beautiful carpets and oriental furniture, the current occupiers having lived and served in India. In the master bedroom, above the bed, there was a beautiful religious triptych of the life of Christ and on the dressing table a fine mother-of-pearl crucifix. I commented on how lovely they were.

"Are you a Catholic?" the woman enquired with a smile.

"I am," I said. "We were married in St Coleman's. We are looking for a family house to bring our children up in."

Her face lit up. "Do you have a family?"

"Not yet," said John, "but we are working on it."

She beamed at us. "We will certainly give you first refusal. We have had some *awful* people come to look at the house. We couldn't possibly have sold our lovely home to them. But you seem ideal."

On the way home I laughed, "I am very pleased you didn't play the sympathy card and tell her about my ectopic."

"It wouldn't have made any difference. Don't you see? They want to sell it to *us*. You're a Catholic and we are looking for a family house. It meets everybody's needs."

We had so fallen in love with the house that even when we went back for a second look and saw that the large family kitchen and the rather small bathroom were the only two rooms with radiators in them, we were not deterred. We were assured that the large fire in the drawing room "draws very well", that there was very little heat loss "because the walls are so thick" and also that the rather untidy half-acre garden was "really no problem to look after". This was unsurprising, as on several occasions we saw an aged retainer known as "Nanny" sweeping the long drive and weeding the two flowerbeds in front of the house.

When our offer to buy was accepted, the owners kindly invited us for sherry to meet our neighbours, a charming gesture. I noticed that there was a paraffin heater burning in the circular hall.

"It throws out wonderful heat in the centre of the house," was the urbane comment. For a fleeting moment I remembered Poole and closed my eyes, but I thought this place would be big enough to cope with a little water vapour.

There were other wonderful discoveries. The house had vast attics and equally enormous cellars with, to John's delight, wine bins with capacity for about 5,000 bottles and what had once been a beer cellar with a barrel chute, although now closed off. Beyond the kitchen was what we thought had been the housekeeper's accommodation: a living room/kitchen with large bedroom above and a rather shabby little bathroom. It was ideal for our tenant, who came with us.

We moved in August 1975. We had so little furniture to take with us, leaving most of the stuff behind in our old house for the tenants that we were moving in to replace us, that we hired a van and did it all ourselves. The vendors said apologetically that they had left some furniture in the cellar and would we mind getting rid of it to the charity War on Want?

"Please," I said, grimacing with what I hoped was appealing desperation, "please may we keep it? We have so little of our own stuff, not even a kitchen table and certainly not a dining room one, or chairs in fact." To this day we still have the large square table with the barleycorn twist legs in the kitchen and the charming oak-framed upholstered sofa that sits so comfortably in the alcove.

Without the stuff salvaged from the cellar, we would have rattled around like peas in a drum. They had left a gas cooker, which had seen better days but was functional all the same. I was disappointed that they had taken the kitchen airer that had been so neatly suspended from the eleven-foot ceiling, and which I had eyed with pleasure. About a week later I was phoned to ask if I would like it back, as the ceilings in our vendors' new home were too low! I accepted with alacrity.

To our pleasure we found that all the deep window embrasures housed the original shutters. They had been screwed shut and then painted over, an act of vandalism that appalled us. One of the first things we did was to unscrew them and carefully prise them open. They worked perfectly. Prior to moving in we had been given the names of the workmen that the previous owners had used. We were assured they could turn their hands to anything; they were apparently "real gems". Appalling examples of their work were found everywhere, although the shutters were probably the worst. We coined the expression "gemmery" to describe their work. We were particularly glad of the shutters, as apart from the drawing room, where they had been left, we had no curtains at all and would certainly have provided entertainment for the local population had we not been so far from the road.

Our neighbour in the other half of the house was a retired child psychologist, a widow. She was delightfully cheerful and friendly. We told her about our adoption plans and she was encouraging, although warned us that we could be in for a long wait, which depressed me. She explained that there were fewer and fewer babies put up for adoption.

"Single mothers are encouraged to keep them," she told us, "which in my opinion is not necessarily a good thing. It's a hard furrow to plough, bringing up a child on your own."

She didn't strike us as being cynical about life but she was certainly realistic. She told us she was treating or counselling the youngsters from the same families that she had treated a generation before. She knew all about the cycle of deprivation. Her face looked very familiar and we soon learned that her brother was the actor Rupert Davies, who played the original detective Maigret in the 1960s television programme of the same name. She looked just like him.

The first month or so we did little, except learn how to live in and enjoy such a spacious place. We soon discovered the drawbacks. The lighting was gloomy and old fashioned, relying in the main on a central pendant. In such large rooms, when you moved away from the down beam, you were in the gloom. In order to provide necessary light, we were forced to surround ourselves with trailing leads and endless table lamps. The power circuits were very basic; in the kitchen there were only two electricity sockets. We also discovered, to our dismay, that the lantern roof above the circular hall leaked. I found this really distressing; our beautiful home that we were so proud of was not watertight.

"It's an old house," said my pragmatic husband. "Old houses leak. Look at Longleat."

We had visited that magnificent pile shortly after moving into The Old Rectory and had noticed the water stains on some of the gilded ceilings. Since then, when visiting stately homes, I have always tended to look upwards. While others are commenting on the boulle armoire and ormolu chiffoniers and enthusing over the Aubusson rugs, I raise my head, peer at the corners and mutter, "Ah, they've got a problem there. Probably a hole in a lead gully somewhere." I find it rather comforting.

As it was summer the heating was not an issue, but we knew there would be a problem later on. We ordered coal in preparation and added to a log pile in the garden; we hoped that the fire would indeed draw well.

One bleak November day I left work early with something I knew was worse than a cold. By the time I reached home I was lightheaded and shivering, with a raging temperature. I thought, *I must get the fire on, or I'll freeze to death before John gets home.*

I staggered out to the garden to find kindling and logs, and eventually got a blaze going. It did draw well and the room warmed. My husband found me, wrapped in a blanket, lying on the sofa, shuddering with fever.

"I promise you, Tiny," he said as he cuddled me and fed me aspirin and a hot toddy, "we'll have central heating throughout the house next winter."

"I certainly hope so." I spoke through chattering teeth. "We might well have a baby."

The next day he brought a letter up to the bedroom. Our adoption application had been approved and we were invited to attend a series of preparatory meetings, starting the following week.

CHAPTER 25

The Investigative Process

Social Services departments tend to be housed in particularly unappealing buildings. John's view was that it was deliberate. In order to discourage claimants from turning up, the whole place was made as unappealing as possible. Our local centre was no exception; built of harsh red brick, the facade had no redeeming features and the wooden window frames were badly in need of a paintbrush. The gravel path to the front door was littered with cigarette butts and sweet wrappers. The front page of the local paper was caught under a coarse doormat and had been trampled to a muddy rag. A Kentucky Fried Chicken carton sat defiantly on a window sill.

We rang the bell and waited apprehensively. Inside was little better. It was very institutional, a gloomy passage painted cream and green, brown lino on the floor. A pleasant, bearded young man showed us into a warm but bleak room. There was a circle of haphazard seats, a mixture of armchairs and wooden upright ones, a large vase of dried flowers on a table by the window (always a sign that desperate measures are being taken to try and brighten a soulless atmosphere) and, incongruously, a television. There was a utilitarian looking coffee table in front of a fire place, and on it, unnervingly, half a dozen boxes of Kleenex tissues. Were they expecting tears? The room was lit by fluorescent strip lights, which cast a pale greenish gloom over everything. There were three other couples standing awkwardly in the middle of the room. Nobody spoke, although we all nodded uneasily at each other.

"We are just waiting for two more couples," our bearded host told us cheerfully. "Why don't you all sit down! I'm Martin, by the way."

I saw that nobody wanted the armchairs, which I thought odd; perhaps they were afraid of feeling too comfortable. When the others had made their choices, we sank down gratefully. Eventually the late arrivals turned up and the meeting got underway.

This, we were told, was just the preliminary meeting to explain the format of what was to follow, and would also allow us to see that we were all facing the same problem. This bland statement I thought quite extraordinary, and mentally I raised my eyebrows. Everybody's problems were different, surely, because we were all different. I was reminded of Tolstoy's view that all happy families are the same, but all unhappy ones are different in their own particular way.

I looked around at the faces of those seated so uneasily in the circle; stress and anxiety was written on every one. Probably I looked the same. John was composed but pale. I was filled with a dull horror and wondered if I was going to be able to cope. We all sat in silence.

Martin seemed to find this unnerving and his voice became a little shaky. I wondered how often he'd done this; perhaps it was his first time. He rushed on into more explanation. We would have the whole adoption procedure explained to us, and the various stages that we would be going through. These group meetings would be followed by individual personal interviews. At the group meetings we would be told about problems associated with adoption. He stressed, I felt rather threateningly, that these were many and varied. We would be asked why we wanted to adopt and then told of the various options open to us. Some prospective parents were willing, indeed happy, to adopt handicapped children (that was the expression used in the seventies). Certainly we would be told about the *kind* of children available for adoption.

"You are all here because you are not able to have children of your own. Infertility is an issue for you all, and we will be talking about that."

I heard a gasp and what I thought was a stifled protest from one of the women. Martin leaned forward, took a packet of tissues from the coffee table, and handed it to her with a smile that I think he thought was understanding and reassuring but which managed to look both insincere and perfunctory.

Before he could speak again one of the men, who I thought might be in his mid-forties or even a well-preserved fifty, cleared his throat and said, "Actually, infertility is not a problem for us. We have three children, teenagers, but we would like to give a home to another child. Should we not come to the meeting on infertility?"

This threw our young social worker into some confusion; he rustled his papers and blushed fiercely. "I'll have to find out about that… I'm really not sure."

"No, it's fine. We don't mind coming if the others don't mind." He looked around at us all.

Avoiding each other's eyes, we nodded or smiled or coughed behind our hands.

"We'll come if you think we should. I just don't think," he added gently, nodding at Martin, "that you should make assumptions about why we are all here."

On the way home in the car I began to laugh out of relief at having escaped from this grisly event, and almost at once John laughed too. "Was that grim, or was that grim? We've got four weeks of this." I enumerated the topics.

"Five: you've forgotten the one about infertility!"

"They aren't going to get much from me. It's ridiculous; it's all in the doctor's letter. I don't want to hear why some other poor soul can't grow her own. I think the couple who have their own kids already are going to give Martin a hard time; don't you?"

"I look forward to it," said my husband.

We attended the meetings dutifully, primed with a very serious gin and tonic beforehand and needing another one afterwards, but there were occasions when we were dismayed by the superficiality of it all. We had filled in so many forms, answered so many questions and read so many pamphlets and booklets that the meetings seemed pointless. Some people, I knew, found them much more difficult than others. There is not unreasonably a certain reticence about speaking in public to strangers about painful episodes or personal failures.

The group discussion on infertility was brought forward "to get it out of the way". It was not surprisingly a stressful meeting and one or two people became heated. By week three, two couples had dropped out. I bumped into one of the girls in town one afternoon. We greeted each other pleasantly. To my question about why she had stopped going, she replied, to my distress, "We aren't like you and John. We can't talk like you. You were both so confident; we felt that it would go against us that we couldn't speak out."

I was horrified and tried to say that gobbiness was not a prerequisite for motherhood. I brought this episode up at the next meeting. Motherhood, I was told repressively, is very stressful, as is the whole adoption procedure; if someone couldn't cope with the meetings, they were going to have problems later on. I felt angry and was ready for an argument, but John patted my knee warningly.

"No point in getting up their noses," he pointed out under cover of a general murmur of opinions, "and they may be right."

This episode had a happy ending though. A few months later the same girl that I had bumped into in town turned up at the antenatal clinic proudly and happily pregnant, and was able to say to me, "Oh, you poor thing; are you still waiting?"

"Probably talking too much," I laughed, and was glad for her.

Some couples had strangely rigid views about children and how they should be brought up, particularly when the issue of the children's background was raised. The need to keep them on the "straight and narrow" was mentioned very firmly by the older pair, who also declared, with some considerable vehemence, that they had never had the slightest personal problem during their adolescence and found it puzzling that so many people seemed to have found it a time of uncertainty and insecurity.

It allowed John one of his better moments. Our bearded social worker leaned forward anxiously, clearly ready to take this issue further. He spoke slowly and intensely: "You know, of course, that most of the babies and indeed the older children placed for adoption are illegitimate… from unmarried mothers, I should say," he corrected himself hastily. "What will you think when your thirteen-year-old daughter starts staying out late, obviously up to mischief, perhaps with boys? Will you think, 'Oh dear, she's taking after her natural mother'?"

"Not at all," said my husband, grinning at me. "I shall obviously assume that she's taking after her adoptive mother."

There was a gasp and a shout of laughter. I tried to look prim, but it was too much and I joined in with the others.

Shortly after that the group meetings finished and we then waited for the individual interviews, which would take place at home.

CHAPTER 26

Esme

The spring of 1976 was dry and fine, and as summer approached, a heatwave swept over the country. Particularly in the south, there was day after glorious day of sunshine. Normally in England, no matter how hot the day, when the sun goes down it becomes chilly; not that year. We sat out in a garden rocker on the terrace in front of the house until 10 or 11 p.m., only stirring to get another beer or glass of wine. In front of us, beyond the Farlington Marshes, the Solent was inky black, and beyond the water the lights of Ryde on the Isle of Wight winked enticingly at us.

We were deeply content. The grim adoption procedure meetings were behind us. There were one or two more hoops to be jumped through, but we felt we were on the home straight. We had a wonderful house, whose roof, temporarily at any rate, didn't leak any more. Thanks to family and friends, we had managed to furnish it with basics so that every bedroom had at least a bed, and the drawing room contained comfortable chairs.

We began to invite several couples at a time to stay and had fabulous, relaxed and cheerful parties. We had no table in the dining room, but thanks to John remembering how his family had coped at various family celebrations, we set up trestles with planks, which I covered with newspaper and white sheets. Candles in the charming Victorian candlesticks my mother-in-law had given me and tea-lights floating in glass bowls made an enchanting display and I was quite glad of the gloomy central pendant, which provided background light to the romantic, glimmering candles.

From our old house John had brought with him a very fine cellar of excellent wine. My local butcher, finding my enthusiasm a spur, provided me with large cuts of very inexpensive meat that he couldn't get rid of elsewhere. "You are," he told me, "the brisket queen of Portsmouth." It was a joint that made the most succulent pot roast imaginable. I also became very inventive and cooked ox heart, trimmed and cut into chunks, in red wine like boeuf bourgignon and defied anybody to know the difference. It was very cheap and a hundred per cent muscle, but cooked slowly was delicious. Two French boys who lodged with us on an educational two-week stay in Portsmouth – and declared they only ate the finest meat – were fooled and refused to believe that the casserole they had eaten with relish was anything other than sirloin.

Not all my culinary initiatives were successful. I once had a disaster with conger eel. I had enticed friends down from London, promising them a fish supper. I planned to cook a whole cod, only to discover that the fish merchant down at the harbour had sold out. He must have seen me coming.

"I've got conger eel. That's got lovely white flesh – good as cod really, cheaper and meatier."

"Right, I'll have one of them."

"A whole one?" he asked doubtfully. "You'd better have a look." He disappeared into the warehouse and returned a few moments later with it slung over his shoulder, a hook through its mouth. It was well over eight feet long, the head about the size of an Alsatian's. I bought a thick middle section. The fish kettle that I bought cost three times as much as the fish.

I had no idea how to cook conger and imagined that I could do what I usually did with salmon or indeed cod: cook it in the oven with herbs and white wine. Conger is good eating, but it has a thick gelatinous layer beneath the very tough skin and needs careful preparation. My dish was almost inedible. It smelled good, but the grey fatty layer under the skin was repulsive to look at and nauseating to taste. My friends made a gallant effort, but we gave up in the end and made do with cheese and pudding.

In June we were notified of the date for the individual adoption interviews. I felt I would be more in control in my own home and therefore I anticipated being relaxed about it. This was, after all, our territory. I was wrong.

We were interrogated separately by a pleasant, mature, quietly spoken man. He talked to John first. I cowered in the kitchen, resisting alcohol, as I needed a clear head.

About an hour later, John came to find me. "Your turn." He smiled reassuringly, which actually unnerved me.

Sitting on my own sofa, I still felt as if I were being interviewed for a very important job, which of course I was. All through the interview, my interrogator made brief notes in a little leather-covered notebook.

His questions were not trivial. What did I feel about family life; how did I envisage it? He asked very personal questions about my own upbringing, about my relationship with my parents and my brother. In many ways I found this interview harder and more troubling than the group ones. It forced me to recall incidents from my childhood that had caused me pain: my father's occasional harshness; my mother's mental fragility; the relative instability of my family life.

He expressed horror that I should have been sent to boarding school aged five, and was even more alarmed that I had been happy and contented there, which he clearly saw as unnatural. He obviously felt that the dynamic of my own family had been dysfunctional, and to some degree it was. He asked if I intended to send my own children, assuming Social Services gave me any, to boarding school and nodded his approval when I said with some vehemence, "Certainly not!" Then he asked me, with what I thought was studied casualness, if I intended to continue working after adopting a child. I felt that a lot hung on this answer, so replied diffidently that I thought it might be difficult, and again he nodded and made a note.

He then began to ask quite personal questions about my relationship with John. Did we ever quarrel? What did we quarrel about? How did we resolve things that we were in disagreement about? Did I consider John an affectionate loving partner? What did I think his views of parenthood were? Did I think he would be a good father? How did I get on with his family and he with mine?

Then out of the blue… Did I consider we had a normal sex life? At this point I offered him a gin and tonic. He smiled and thanked me, but refused. Considering that this might give me breathing space, I threw caution to the winds and poured myself a large one, then sat down, taking a deep breath. "I tell you what," I said. "You define a normal sex life and I'll tell you if we have one." He smiled and made another note, but didn't elaborate.

He asked politely to see the house, downstairs and up: bedrooms, bathroom, kitchen, everywhere. John said afterwards that he wanted to see if we had any "kinky" stuff lying around. Somehow I rather doubted that, but there were apocryphal stories about social workers peering into lavatory cisterns and even asking deeply personal questions about particular sexual practices.

Before he left, he said something that impressed me: "Our job as social workers is not to provide babies or children for childless couples; it is to provide happy, well-balanced families for the infants in our care. We are not here to remedy whatever issue of infertility you might have. The children are the issue, and that is to find loving homes for them."

Eventually we received official notification that we had passed all the tests, although I think it was expressed differently. We had met all the criteria and were now officially on the prospective adopters' register.

"What now?" I said, turning the letter over and over in my hand.

John's reply was calm. "We wait; we just have to be patient."

We were emotionally exhausted and felt we needed a break, so in August, with the summer heat at its most intense, we went to East Anglia on holiday. The family had two shabby old caravans on a very primitive site in Walberswick, a large, wealthy and attractive village on the coast. It had everything a village could want: an ancient ruined church, a shop and two pubs, both of which sold Adnams beer, considered at least by the locals as the very nectar of life. There were coastal walks, a long pebble beach with sand at low tide and the North Sea, which made for adventurous bathing. The vans were old but comfortable. For all of John's life this had been a holiday destination, and he loved it.

Walberswick village was a no through road, and to get anywhere you needed a car, but there was an alternative. We walked round the lanes and across the village green down to the harbour, where Bob the ferryman, for 20p, would row his boat across the mouth of the River Blyth to the Blackshore, so that we could walk along the footpath. This was lined with fronds of fennel and the coarser alexanders, and we would go through the field to Southwold, a small, quintessentially English seaside resort. It was a town that seemed caught in a fifties time warp. Many of the shops closed at 12:30 and didn't open again till 2 p.m. If we got our timing wrong, we were forced to sit in a pub, of which there were an extraordinary number, all selling Adnams and all owned by the brewery, itself situated in the very centre of the town. It was astonishing how often we managed to arrive in Southwold just as the shops were closing!

We had a delightful break, sleeping, eating, drinking, swimming and walking. The past year and a half had been dreadful, but in that bucolic environment some calm and sense of wellbeing returned.

Back at work the hospital and the helpful sympathy of my colleagues was a great support. I was also very lucky in my sister-in-law Annie, who began to pass baby equipment over to me. She and Ed had two little boys, but she had plenty of unisex stuff to pass on. They arrived one evening with a huge Silver Cross pram. The handle was well above my waist height, so it was a bit high for me, but I liked the idea of something handed down from family to family. Annie had it second-hand from a friend, so I never considered turning it down.

They also brought a little oak rocking crib, and John and I began to kit out the smallest bedroom as a nursery. It was very difficult to know what to buy as we didn't know what we were going to get. There wasn't much point in buying baby grows for a newborn if we were to be presented with a two-year-old.

Summer slid definitively into autumn and after months of drought the rain came. For many it was a relief, although I was sad to see the end of those hot days and wonderful balmy evenings. We had central heating installed in the house so we wouldn't be dependent on the open fires and were generally settled and comfortable. Then stunningly, one evening, when thoughts of the baby had become a sort of pleasant but not urgent expectation, the phone rang.

A young woman said, "It's about your adoption application. We have a baby that we think you might like to see. She's a little girl, ten weeks old, and is currently with a short-term foster family in Portsmouth. Are you free tomorrow?"

I heard the words but couldn't take them in. I had to ask her to repeat it all, and then wanted to shout, *Tomorrow? TOMORROW? Why not tonight? Can we see her tonight?* I didn't, and was astonished at my control.

"Yes, that would be wonderful. Where and when? Hang on, let me tell my husband." I covered the mouthpiece. "They've got a baby for us! A baby!"

John put his arms around me, and I felt his breath against my head. "Wonderful! Oh, wonderful, Tiny."

We stood, our heads pressed together, to listen to the instructions. We were given an address and a time, and arranged to meet this wonderful bringer of good news, yet another different social worker, at the foster home the next day.

I was astonished at how soundly I slept that night. "Just as well," observed my practical husband. "If we bring her home with us today, it will be the last unbroken night we'll have for some time!"

We waited outside the foster home for the social worker. I had a sudden moment of panic as I saw her car draw up.

"What if I don't like it?"

"Whatever do you mean? Why on earth wouldn't you like it?"

"If it's got a head like a turnip…" my voice tailed off. Not all babies are beautiful; indeed, I'd seen some so plain that only a mother's love would find it even vaguely attractive.

John took my hand and said firmly, "You'll be fine. It's all going to be fine."

I found I was trembling with excitement, my mouth dry and

my hands cold with apprehension. The house was warm but noisy. There seemed to be several small children running about and a radio was playing loudly somewhere. The social worker smiled brightly and said, "Ah, here she is." The baby was wrapped in a shawl but her head, which was uncovered, was completely bald and a perfectly beautiful sphere. I saw a small face with enormous blue eyes. She was gorgeous, having lost the wrinkled, rather red skin of the newborn. Her complexion was opalescent.

"Would you like to hold her?"

I felt the small body against me and asked inanely, "What does she weigh?" I couldn't trust my voice to say more. She smelled of talcum powder and newness and of everything I had ever yearned for and wanted. Her little shell nails were miraculous. She curled her fingers tightly around my thumb and I wanted to cry with joy. Against the light her ears were transparent. The down on her head was feather soft. I couldn't believe it. I, who had seen so many hundreds of babies, was sure I had never seen one this perfect, this magical – because she would soon be ours.

I passed her to John, who held her wordlessly for a moment against his shoulder. Then he ran his hand gently over her head. "This feels so lumpy!"

"Lumpy?" I was bemused. "Oh, I see. It's because the fontanelles, the soft bits, are not fully closed. You can feel the edges of her skull bones, but it's normal. She's perfect!"

"Not quite," said the foster mother. "She's got one ear that's just a little smaller than the other. It will probably sort itself out, but if it doesn't she can always cover it with her hair."

"Assuming she grows any." John had got his emotions under control again and was back to his normal ironic self. I wasn't fooled though; I'd seen the tears in his eyes.

"Tomorrow you might like to come and bath and feed her." The foster mother was smiling at me.

I felt a rush of dismay. "Aren't we taking her today?"

"Oh! I think you need time to get to know each other. And I imagine you have some shopping to do: bottles and nappies at least."

We knew she was right, but the disappointment was keen. It was an effort to hand her back.

"Mothercare, I think," announced John as we drove away. The foster mother had kindly given us a list so we had a clearer idea of what we needed and we spent a couple of hours in the Portsmouth branch.

"Basics!" recommended John, but I was like a child in a toy shop. Some of the clothes were irresistible.

"Oh, darling! Wouldn't she look lovely in this?"

"Yes, she would, but it's baby grows we need and nappies, and cot sheets and blankets and all the other paraphernalia – I don't know, cream and cleaning stuff, oh and little jackets and something padded and warm for when we take her out in that ridiculous *perambulator*."

Over the next three days I went to bath and feed the baby and then at last we brought her home. She slept in the car and then, when John brought the carrycot into the kitchen, opened her eyes and promptly began to yell. I was astonished at the volume of noise. Neither of us cared. We took it in turns to hold her and rock her, and then I prepared a bottle and fed her, and she slept again.

We named her Esme Jane: Esme being my mother-in-law's second name and Jane after my grandmother. Now, finally, we were a family.

Chapter 27

Conflict

As soon as we were notified by Social Services that there was a possible baby for us, I had gone to see Matron to say that I needed some compassionate leave to organize myself. I took a few days. When Esme was placed with us, I went back, this time with my baby, to show her off to my colleagues, who all seemed delighted for me, and to see Matron again to discuss my situation.

Initially this all seemed to be going quite well. Then she asked, "When will you be handing in your notice?" She was perfectly pleasant but I was taken aback.

"I don't know. It's six weeks before the preliminary adoption papers can be signed by the baby's natural mother. She can change her mind and ask for the baby to be returned to her. I don't think she will: I pray that she won't. But it could happen and then I would have no baby and no job!"

"Well," she said, "why don't you take another couple of weeks and we'll look at it then."

"Miss Upman, I don't think you understand. Two weeks is not going to cover it. Why can't I have maternity leave?"

She stared at me in astonishment. "You aren't eligible: you haven't been pregnant – well, not with this little infant," she amended hastily. "You haven't given birth; there's just no precedent. I am not rushing you, but currently the clinic is understaffed and I can't fill your post until you resign."

I felt angry and bitter, and John was enraged. The Royal College of Midwives were no real help. They were sympathetic and could see that the time specified for maternity leave, several weeks before birth and several after, could not be applied to me as I had had no idea when the cloak of motherhood would fall upon me. There just wasn't any legislation to cover my situation. The best I could hope for was a month's grace. I should, they said, resign and ask for a month's paid absence.

In desperation I applied to COHSE, the hospital workers' union, for advice. This was viewed with quite marked disapproval by the maternity hierarchy. COHSE told me they could help but it would be quite a battle. On no account should I resign! I didn't relish becoming involved in an industrial dispute at that time, so eventually I handed in my notice and was given a month's pay.

Esme was a source of immense joy, but motherhood was very draining. We had disturbed nights, which was normal, but instead of being sensible and snoozing during the day when she was asleep, I was rushing around washing nappies (no disposable ones in those days) and doing my best to keep the house in order. In the main she was a good baby and spent more time chuckling to herself, sucking her toes, looking around with her enormous blue eyes and seeming to find the world a great source of amusement, than crying. The only exception was at night. She was very slow to settle and howled ceaselessly. I paced round and round the gallery until she fell asleep on my shoulder.

One evening, in despair, I phoned her foster mother. I was very nearly in tears myself.

"I can't understand why she won't go to sleep. She sleeps in her pram outside, she sleeps in the car, she even falls asleep on the sofa in the kitchen, and goodness knows that's noisy enough, but in a nice, quiet, dark nursery, she's shouting till 10 p.m."

"Ah well," said this good lady, "I think that's your problem. Here, she slept in her pram under the stairs. The light was on, the other children were racing around up and down stairs, the TV was on – all the noise you can imagine. Leave the light on and put a radio in her room."

I followed this excellent piece of advice and found that my baby daughter was just as happy to fall asleep to the shipping forecast as she was to *The Archers* or even *Just a Minute*. She would probably have loved *Top of the Pops*. It was noise and not quietness that she liked.

The adoption procedure was still grinding on and not always smoothly. The guardian ad litem appointed to ensure that Esme was in good hands was charming and helpful, but some of the later social workers that we dealt with were very autocratic. When the moment to finalize the papers came, we turned up again at the grim soulless office that we had begun to detest. Two social workers that we had never met before presented us with a form detailing all our particulars and with space for those of Esme's natural mother. In brackets it said "For the information of the adopters", but this space was blank. We were quite unprepared for what followed.

"No, no," we were told when John queried this. "We don't fill this in – in the interests of confidentiality."

"But it says it's for *our* information! Half the information on this form is missing. You can't submit it like that."

"No, of course not. We *do* fill it in, but confidentially. You must just trust us."

"I tell you what," said John, white with fury. "You write me a blank cheque and I promise you I won't cash it. You'll just have to trust me."

"You are being very foolish." The voice was bland but the tight-lipped expression was threatening. I had never felt so vulnerable. My stomach, always a weak point, churned and I felt a rush of acidity.

Then the second social worker said quietly, "Perhaps you don't really want this baby." It was so blatantly a threat that I actually laughed, although I could have just as easily thrown up.

John took a deep breath. I could see him struggling. "We want this baby very much indeed, more than anything in fact, but I am not signing a form where information meant for us is missing. When we see that information, we'll sign. You'd better go and talk to someone higher up the chain of command."

We refused to budge and there was a stand-off. We left the office with our baby, the forms unsigned. I was filled with dread.

Without the forms being signed and registered, we had no rights at all. Our baby could be taken away at any time and we had no recourse to anything.

The whole episode was deplorable. Obviously a pattern had been established by the social workers. They had decided, irrespective of the law, that in the interests of "confidentiality" there were some things they would choose not to reveal. This was probably a purely local thing, but for all I knew half the local authorities in Great Britain were making independent decisions about a great many things, contrary to general legislation.

Christmas was upon us and we sweated through the festivities, gritting our teeth and agonizing from day to day. Ed and Annie invited everybody for Christmas dinner and were quietly supportive. Annie gave me lots of thing to do to keep me occupied and to try to prevent me from brooding. We kept the situation from Mum and Dad, knowing how distressed they would be, but it was a terrible time. Fury, anguish, despair and fear were all mixed up with an overwhelming helplessness. The whole episode was an exercise in the arbitrary wielding of power. We began to wonder whom we could appeal to.

Then suddenly, unexpectedly and with no explanation of the change in their procedure, they rolled over. After the Christmas break we received the completed forms in the post, with a civil covering letter asking us to sign and return them. There was no mention of what had gone before. What was extraordinary was how anodyne the information that had been withheld from us actually was: a name, an age, an ethnic status, a date of birth, the place of Esme's birth. Nothing else: no address, no telephone number, no national insurance number – nothing that would identify this young woman without considerably more effort.

The guardian ad litem completed her supervision and we waited for the court appointment that would finalize everything. Eventually we were summoned, and one cold March day we turned up at court for the full adoption order. Esme looked enchanting in her white lacy dress and pink tights. She was six months old, still as dainty as ever, and still as bald. I was always careful to keep her head warm, as John, with less and less hair on *his* head, was always complaining about heat loss. I had put a little pink and white mob cap on her, which she resented and kept trying to pull off. She would hook her finger under the elastic and tug away with a greater or lesser degree of success. Her very fetching appearance was spoiled by her final effort: as we were walking into the judge's chambers she had managed to pull it down over one eye, the other cerulean blue one swivelling balefully.

"She looks like a drunken dowager," hissed John. It was such an apt description that I began to laugh. The judge, looking at us, began to laugh too. He was a rotund, jolly-looking man with pink cheeks, a frill of white hair and a warm smile. He didn't look in the least like a judge.

Without any preamble he said, "I am very happy to grant this adoption order. This is a truly nice way for me to start my day, making people happy. From the moment I sign this, you stand in the same relationship to this little girl as if you were her natural parents, and she your natural child. You will have the same joy, pain, worry and pleasure as any other parent; oh, and the same expenses too!"

And so with that we had our daughter, and all the fatigue, anguish and worry melted away in the glow of our triumph and success.

Chapter 28

Intermission

We weren't very sure about whether we should apply to adopt another child straight away. If we were considered good adopters, and the aim of the Social Services adoption department was to find good parents for their children, then we were ideal candidates. At least we thought so! However, all registered adopters, in theory, were ideal candidates, and given the limited number of infants available for adoption we thought the department might prioritize those who were still on the waiting list.

My mother-in-law, with her usual calm good sense and sensitivity, encouraged us to wait a little. "You need time to get to know your little girl. I think she is entitled to have you both to herself for a little. Don't you?"

Mum was a doting grandmother, and Dad, although he felt babies were a woman's thing, was almost as captivated. Esme was a happy child, very smiley and willing to go to anybody, which made getting a babysitter easy. But she was adventurous and was on her feet and walking at nine months, so I had to be vigilant. Climbing out of her cot was a breeze for her, but at least we could contain her in her bedroom.

The rest of the house was problematic. John taught her to go up and down stairs on the principle that if she learned how to do it she would be less likely to fall. Later, but not much later, and to my apprehension, she mastered the wooden ladder down to the cellar. She seemed to me a brave little girl. Nothing alarmed or frightened her, except a scrubbing brush that she came across in a kitchen cupboard. It was on its back, the long, stiff, brown bristles uppermost. She recoiled with a cry of terror, and clung to my knees. What primordial fear had surfaced there, I wondered? I had to get rid of it in the end, as despite my gentle explanation – "It's just a brush, darling; just an old brush" – she showed the same reaction every time she came across it.

She was fascinated by the woodlice that despite my best efforts still found their way into the kitchen. She would pursue them across the floor. Then with her index finger and thumb, like a pincer, she would pick them up and, if I wasn't quick enough, pop them into her mouth with obvious relish and crunch them.

"They are only filled with wood." I didn't find John's reassurance in the least consoling. I later discovered that they ate considerably more than wood and actually processed dead organic matter, which meant that they ate anything rotten that came their way. But it didn't seem to do her any harm. Eventually, once she was permanently on her feet, she found other more interesting things to pursue.

My own parents seemed delighted with this new little person in their lives, but as my father lived near Oxford and my mother in Brighton, neither of them were very involved with her. Even had they lived closer I don't think they would have been very hands-on. They were pleased with the idea of grandchildren, but at a distance. Actually my mother showed an irritating but not unexpected tendency to jealousy if I was ever distracted in conversation with her by the needs or demands of my baby daughter. "Honestly," she expostulated, "it's useless talking to you when that child's around. I can't get any sense out of you at all."

I discussed this with Di, who lived close by. She had a little boy, Richard, about nine months older than Esme. The two little ones played well together and there wasn't too much fighting, despite the predominance of Fisher-Price toys, which Esme adored but thought were mainly for bashing things with. Often Richard's head got in the way, but he was a placid and friendly child and tears didn't come too often.

Over coffee I told her, "My mother's never been easy, but this behaviour really jars."

Di sighed. "My mother's the same. They just find it hard not coming first any more. She really resents it. I mean she loves Richard, thinks he's lovely, but… she's very much of the 'kids should be seen and not heard' generation, and kids are noisy and claim your attention. If you don't pay them attention they tend to wander off, probably into the kitchen to pull heaven knows what down on their heads. There are only so many times you can say, 'Just wait. Mummy's talking to Granny.'"

This issue was a topic of conversation whenever I met any friends with small babies; Di was not the only one. Several of my ex-colleagues from the hospital had had children around the time we had Esme and almost all of them had experienced the same periodic resentment and jealousy scenario. I could only be profoundly grateful that I had a mother-in-law who was everybody's idea of the perfect grandmother.

Mum, on the other hand, related to children in an extraordinarily sensitive and intimate way. She had an instinctive understanding of how they functioned and even of their subconscious needs. She never forced herself on them but was always ready to accommodate herself to their wants. If Esme wanted to play with the kitchen scales, or the pots and pans, or pour dried pasta or rice from one bowl to another, or look at the toys and baby clothes in the Freeman's catalogue, or tuck her dolls into a kitchen drawer and make a bed for them with tea towels; if she wanted to potter with her granny in the garden, pick dandelions and indeed anything else she fancied, make daisy-chains, gather pebbles, then it all happened very simply and easily. As she grew older, Mum took her on the bus down to the harbour and across on the Gosport ferry: a real adventure! Esme adored her.

We had never hidden the fact that our daughter was an adopted child, a precious, very special baby. It was spoken of openly and with pride. When we took her to Walberswick, occasionally people who didn't know us would comment about how much she looked liked me. I realized it is the sort of thing people say to young mothers and was amused. Their embarrassment when I said that Esme was adopted was patent. "It's not a secret," I used to say. "Esme will grow up knowing that she came to us as a chosen child."

Curiously, although there was no genetic link at all, as she grew up she began to develop marked physical similarities to the Richardsons. She could have passed for Ed's daughter. She was tall, with fine pale skin and fair hair. She saw James and Oliver, her cousins, frequently, and the "sibling" resemblance was marked. They were extremely fond of their little cousin and very gentle with her.

In March 1978, when she was eighteen months old, we applied to adopt another child. Esme was thrilled. Even as a very little girl she was enthralled by babies. "Will the baby come soon?" It was a daily question, and she was profoundly dissatisfied with my reply: "Poppet, I just don't know."

Having faced all the hurdles the first time around, we expected it would be much less traumatic, and indeed the whole process initially was much easier. There were no more investigations to be done, just an acknowledgment of our application, and a note advising us that there was a wait of about six months. When they had a suitable child, we would be notified.

"Very bureaucratic. Six months, eh? I don't think we should hold our breath," said John sourly. "And don't tell Esme."

"I expect you'll want a boy this time. It's nice to have the choice." John's abrasive godmother was on one of her periodic visits to Mum and Dad's. I considered this remark in poor taste, so replied tersely that in fact we didn't have a choice. On our application form we had said we would be delighted with whatever we were offered; we didn't mind what the sex or the ethnic background was and would be perfectly happy with a black child. She raised her eyebrows in what I took to be either astonishment or disbelief but said nothing. She was another spinster lady who viewed John as her special boy and tended to sideline me.

Probably foolishly, we hoped to hear sooner rather than later, but the months drifted on and just after Esme's third birthday in September 1979, John and I went to America for a fortnight's holiday. Mum and Dad came to stay, and Esme, with the realization that she would have her grandparents' undivided attention, let us go with barely a kiss.

We stayed with friends in Boston and then hired a car and drove north through the Adirondacks up as far as the Canadian border. The autumn colours were spectacular, although everyone we met said, "Oh, it's rubbish this year." I found it hard to imagine that this "fall" could be bettered, but I had to take their word for it. I found the Americans delightful: warm and charming. We weren't assailed with demands to tell them when we were going to leave damp, dreary old England and settle in the USA.

They seemed fascinated by all things British, particularly our English accents. On one occasion in a ski lodge bar we chatted to a couple from California. It was my turn to go to the bar. The drinks seemed to me quite exotic so I said to the barman, "You might have to help me here. Now, I would like a Budweiser, a White Russian, a Black Russian, and a glass of white wine – Californian if you've got it. Our American friends here think it's the best."

The barman looked at me smilingly, his head on one side, then said, "Gee, that's pretty, lady. Can you say that all over again?" So laughingly, and just to oblige him, I did.

CHAPTER 29

About the Boy

The holiday was a great success but I missed my little girl, so it was with pleasure and anticipation that we returned home. We found her wrapped in a towel on her granny's knee, fresh, pink and sweet smelling, and warm from her bath. She hugged us with shrieks of pleasure, wrapping damp arms around my neck.

"I shall be so sorry to give her back. She's been so good," Mum beamed at us. "But I think you might need me a little longer. There was a phone call from Social Services today."

Instinctively I looked at my watch. It was gone 6 p.m.

Mum smiled understandingly. "It's too late to phone now: they shut at 5 p.m. It will have to be tomorrow morning. I've got a name for you downstairs."

We did feel a rush of excitement, but that evening we were too involved with Esme to take it in. It was only the next morning, when rather breathlessly I phoned Social Services, it occurred to me that if they did have a child for us, in all likelihood he or she would be in the house before the end of the week.

A young and pleasant voice answered the phone. She introduced herself as Alice X. They had, she said, not a baby but a toddler: a little boy about fifteen months old. They were looking for foster parents with a view to adoption. We were a little taken aback; it was not what we were expecting.

"We are looking for really motivated parents. This little boy's future is not with his mother, so although we are looking for foster parents, it is with a view to adoption."

"Look," I said, "I need to talk this over with my husband. It's a different situation. Anyway, we are not cleared as foster parents. If he is never going back to his mother, what's the hold-up with placing him for adoption straight away?"

"It's because of his age. Really he's little more than a baby, but that's the issue: he is more than a baby; he is much more self-aware. He will need time to adapt and to settle. Why not talk it over and ring me back? I can arrange for you to go and visit him if you want to."

We were excited, but had not prepared for this eventuality. John, always more rational and cautious than me, pointed out that if we went to see this very little boy, we would almost certainly want to take him. "Are we sure we really want to go? It's not like inspecting livestock, is it? Not that I've ever done that! This is a child, not a parcel that you unwrap and then say you don't like the look of and reject."

"Well," I pointed out, "he won't know that he's being inspected. It's we who will have the heartbreak of the decision."

I was wrong, but I didn't know it at the time.

In the evening we phoned back and said we would like to see the child. There was one thing that puzzled me. What, I wanted to know, was wrong with the current foster parents adopting the child themselves?

"We don't think they are suitable," Alice told me blandly.

We found the little boy in a large, pleasant, terraced house. He had soft, light brown hair and hazel eyes and a shy, engaging smile. He came willingly to me and sat on my knee. He was just beginning to talk but then left me to pick up a football, which he dribbled with some expertise around the room. "Football," he said, kicking it toward John.

He was momentarily distracted by a handsome marmalade tabby that strolled into the room.

"He loves Daisy," said the foster mother, "and although she sometimes scratches the others, she's so good with him."

I was in some turmoil. I thought the child, called Paul, was lovely, but he clearly had an attachment to his present home and the familiar things in it. I was going to feel as if I was wrenching him away from everything he knew and loved.

"We think he's lovely," we told Alice, "but we need to think about it just a little more. May we visit him again tomorrow?"

It was agreed that we should come the following lunchtime, give him his meal and perhaps take him out.

He seemed a sweet-natured little boy, if somewhat solemn. I was surprised that he was not even attempting to feed himself. I remembered Esme's refusal when she was just over a year old to be fed by me. Mealtimes were necessarily a messy business, but as usual my daughter was determined to have her own way. Short of putting her head in a vice and handcuffing her hands to her high chair, there was no way I could spoon-feed her. This little fellow opened his mouth like a robin.

I thought he was delightful. We stayed for a couple of hours, playing with him and just watching. Despite my determination to be cautious and even reticent, I could feel huge emotional urgings. I thought of John's warning: if this was a parcel, I loved the contents.

I went along to see Paul the next day and stayed for three or four hours, taking him out for a walk in his pushchair. He seemed a happy little boy, playing contentedly and stroking the very tolerant marmalade cat with evident enjoyment.

"I'm finding this really hard," his foster mother told me. "We wanted to adopt him but they said we hadn't been passed for adoption. We would need to apply, and there was no guarantee..." her voice trailed off.

I didn't know what to say. Her distress seemed so reasonable.

That evening John and I sat down and talked things over. We thought the whole situation ambiguous. We were not approved as foster parents. If Social Services wanted to place the child with us, it had to be as prospective adopters. We had been assured that the boy had no future with his mother, so what was the hold-up?

The next day we rang Alice and said we would like some clarification of the situation. Why had he been removed from his mother, and when? Why was there no possibility of his being returned to her? How long had he been with the present foster family, and why were they considered unsuitable to adopt him when they so clearly wanted to?

"I'll come and see you. How about 7 p.m.? Do you mind me coming out of hours? I expect your little girl will be in bed." She sounded reassuring, but above all she sounded sensible and competent. There were no threats this time.

We sat over coffee in the kitchen and were given all the answers. They were harrowing. At ten months Paul had been theoretically abandoned, his mother leaving him in the care of a fourteen-year-old boy in order to go to a music festival in Bristol. The young adolescent, alarmed after four days by the non-appearance of the baby's mother, took him to the local police station, who called Social Services. As Paul was already on the "At Risk" register because of unexplained burn marks on his hand, Social Services had no option but to find him "a place of safety". The child's mother was considered unfit to have him in her care, as in fact she had given him no care. He had been left alone, strapped into a pushchair, for hours at a time. This information was given to Social Services by irate neighbours, alarmed by persistent crying from the mother's flat.

We listened to this dreadful tale in some distress; it was too awful for tears. The current foster parents were good people, but their own natural children were suffering from a deteriorating genetic condition that was untreatable, and it was felt that their reasons for wanting to adopt Paul were not entirely disinterested. The court order placing him in the supervisory care of Social Services specified "fostering with the view to adoption".

Alice, our social worker, was very persuasive, although I must say we didn't need much persuading. She told us, "This little baby boy needs parents who can give him love, security, safety and happiness." She didn't say, "If you don't want him, I've got other couples who do." After our previous experience with Esme's adoption, I thought other social workers might have done. She continued, "I just think you are both perfect for him," and smiled.

I looked at John, who grinned at us both. "When a pretty blonde girl smiles at you, it's quite difficult to say no!" he said. Alice pretended to look shocked, but failed and smiled back at him.

"I don't think we were hesitating," I said. "We just needed some answers." I looked at my husband for his acknowledgment and he nodded. "Yes please, we would like to go ahead... I mean to take him... I mean... you know, to adopt him."

"I know what you mean." She smiled again. "Today's Thursday. See Paul again tomorrow. Then we will organize a series of visits to you – maybe he could stay overnight and this will reduce the trauma of separation that he's bound to feel. I'll explain the process to his foster family."

After she'd gone we sat in a state of emotional exhaustion. I thought gin would make me cry so had a large glass of wine instead. My husband firmly said he would have coffee, put the kettle on, then weakened and had two beers!

Next day I phoned the foster mother and went to pick her and Paul up in time for lunch. Esme was wild with excitement. It was difficult to explain to her that this was quite a large baby. He was still crawling most of the time, but a football had him on his feet in a trice. I was uncertain as to how she would take to him. Once in the house she calmed down and scampered off to get him some toys. They seemed to be interacting well together. She looked uncertain about my retrieving the high chair from the cellar and putting him into it for his meal, even though she had been out of it for some months. Astonishingly, she wanted me to feed her when she saw me feeding him. I saw this as ominous, but just jollied her along. After our lunch, Paul fell asleep on the sofa. We put a baby blanket over him and I put Esme down for her afternoon nap, in her room.

In the kitchen, with both the children quiet, I began to talk with the foster mother about some access visits and proposed we looked at the week ahead to decide some times. The poor woman seemed increasingly uneasy, but we tentatively agreed some dates. The atmosphere was becoming tense. Her replies to my suggestions were monosyllabic, and I was at a loss to know what to do. It was an enormous relief when John arrived home early, hoping to see Paul before he was taken away again. Both the children woke and I was preoccupied getting drinks for them. John went to change out of his suit. When he came down, he picked Paul up and laughed as he had his beard tugged, Paul chuckling as he did so.

Suddenly we heard, "I can't do it this way. I can't let him go, day by day. You're nice people; he seems happy with you. You take him now. I'll ring my husband. He can come and collect me and bring all his stuff!"

Shocked and startled, John said, "I don't think we can do that. Social Services have a system; we have to go along with it."

"If I say I can't keep him any longer, what can anybody do? They won't want to find another temporary home for him: they'll prefer to leave him with you. It's the best way." She spoke pleadingly, her face stricken. "I'm just going to leave him; you'll have to keep him!"

She fled the kitchen and we heard her on the phone, clearly distraught.

"Is there an emergency number for Social Services?" I asked.

"I'm sure there is, but I don't know it and in a way she's right. What are their options? Insist these poor folk take the little chap home with them? Put him in a foster home over the weekend? It's surely preferable to leave him here."

"I suppose so. Good Lord, I never expected this. What a mess!"

In due course all the clothes and paraphernalia arrived, delivered by an equally distressed foster father. There was a moment when I thought and indeed prayed they might reconsider, but it was a vain hope. She was so distressed, she didn't even kiss the boy goodbye. She gave him a long last look and then they were gone.

We got through the weekend in a state of acute anxiety. Our new son slept well and ate with apparent relish. Esme was no longer in a cot but took a dim view, as she had done with the high chair, of it being reinstated. We watched Paul for signs of distress, but initially, apart from being rather quiet, he seemed contented enough. He played with toys and I began to wonder when he would miss his foster family or appear to notice their absence. One thing I did gradually become aware of was that he avoided looking at me. If I tried to catch his eye and smile, he looked away. He didn't resist being picked up; in fact he came to me if he bumped himself or fell over, but he didn't raise his face to mine and I got no response when I kissed him. John fared better; the beard was a great draw. Paul cried very little and when he did it was a soft, plaintive sound. Sometimes, in those two days, I saw him looking around with what was clearly bewilderment. Everything and everyone he knew and loved had mysteriously disappeared in a flash, in an instant. I was torn by the thought of his anguish as he wondered when they would return and take him home.

Not surprisingly Social Services were horrified when we eventually contacted them to explain what had happened. The fault was not with us, although they clearly felt we should have resisted the pressure to take the child. In the end they were pragmatic about it, taking the view that what was done was done and we should all try to minimize the harm to Paul. I thought they seemed pretty sanguine about the possible effect of such devastating trauma on a baby not yet two. The attitude seemed to be that as he was very young, he would get over it quickly and soon settle down. Many people expressed astonishment that he appeared to be adapting so well and superficially it seemed true, but I was uneasy about the statement.

I felt he had just shut down, a basic instinct for self-preservation; he simply ate and slept. I saw him one morning standing at the French windows in the drawing room. He had his face and little hands pressed against the glass and was murmuring something very quietly. I came to kneel beside him, looked out into the garden and saw that he was watching a ginger cat stroll across the lawn.

"Daisy," he said. "Daisy, Daisy." His eyes were riveted on the animal. Had *she* at least come to find him? It wasn't the cat from his foster home, but just for that moment he thought it was. There was a world of loss and longing in those terrible whispered words. I felt that despite all my good intentions and my ardent desire to make this child happy, in taking him from all he knew and loved I had done something monstrous.

CHAPTER 30

The Calm

If Paul was in turmoil those first few weeks, Esme was also a very troubled little girl. She had wanted, indeed expected, a baby. Perhaps unwisely, that was what we had told her was coming. At first she seemed to be adapting well. Small children have no real concept of the long-term future, so maybe she thought that a time would come when there would be just the three of us again. As time passed and there was no sign of Paul going away, she became resentful and even antagonistic. She guarded her own toys with ferocious possessiveness and claimed his too, for good measure.

One evening when I was changing his nappy, I caught sight of her sullen little face as she stood beside me. Paul was crying: like many babies, he didn't like this nappy-changing business.

"Dear me, he doesn't like this, does he?" I said, trying to lighten the atmosphere. "He's only little."

"He's not little; he's too big," she retorted fiercely. "I wanted a baby." Then she added with more truth than she knew, "He doesn't like it here. He wants to go home."

"Darling," I took a deep breath, "he will learn to love it here, because now this *is* his home. I'm *his* mummy too."

After that, her fury knew no bounds. I couldn't leave them alone together, not even for a moment. I had to explain his black eye and the scratches on his cheeks and chin to Alice. Much to my relief, she saw it as perfectly understandable, pointing out that Esme had wanted a baby and what she got was an instant competitor. "Her pretty little nose is so out of joint it's practically under her ear."

We scolded Esme when she pushed or hit Paul, but it was

difficult, as her own distress was so evident. Eventually, as the weeks passed, she got used to him, and then began to tolerate him and eventually accept him, although it would be several months before she began to like him, never mind love him. However, as the age difference was not so great and they were less than two years apart, the positive side of having a companion to play with eventually outweighed her jealousy, most of the time. But she was still always ready to assert her seniority and to claim the right to have first shot at anything, so we had to be firm with her.

I tried to do something different each day to amuse and entertain them, in order that they weren't locked together in the house. We went to the park or the swimming pool, or to feed the ducks. With two small people, I found motherhood more challenging than I had expected. Because I had so longed for children, I thought I would find it easy and be very good at it. In fact I found it hard work, and decided I wasn't very good at it at all. I wasn't patient enough, and because Esme was such a little toughie and Paul needed so much careful handling, I was in a state of permanent exhaustion. I would get cross quite quickly, and then feel ashamed and guilty. A friend of mine told me that despite absolutely adoring her children, motherhood was the biggest disillusionment of her adult life; a sentiment I had some sympathy with.

Di had a second son, Andrew, in October 1977; her boys were just nineteen months apart. She said she didn't know if having them close together was a good or bad thing. They played well together, but she too confessed to a state of almost permanent fatigue.

"Isn't this all supposed to come naturally?" I asked her crossly one afternoon in her garden, the children playing reasonably happily on the lawn.

"I don't actually think nature's all that clever," she replied. "Look at hurricanes, tearing homes to bits, and trees falling on cars and houses and squashing people flat, not to mention flash floods and lightning strikes, before you move on to rats and spiders! That's nature! What do they say – it's 'red in tooth and claw'? I think 50 per cent of nature is pretty unpleasant and more than a little worrying. We are told that mother love is part of the human condition, whatever that means, but there are moments when I quite dislike my children. I wouldn't be without them for the world, but there's no doubt it's no walk in the park."

I could only agree with her. What I found hardest at that time was Paul's continued reluctance to bond with me. Eye contact was still avoided, and if he glanced at me at all, it was fleetingly. Sometimes I caught a look on his face that I can only describe as an expression of deep and lonely grief; a little boy lost. I found it piercingly sad and would cajole him, "Come to your mummy for a cuddle, my little boy," but he never did. If I picked him up he tolerated it, but showed no real response. Actually, in her robust and lively way, Esme was quite an antidote to his distress, as despite her occasional roughness with him, his face would brighten when she appeared.

Then when he had been with us for about two months, he developed a bad chest infection. He was listless and reluctant to eat, so I became anxious; not a good combination. All that sort of emotional interaction is usually counter-productive in my experience; I knew I was over-protective. The doctor was reassuring, but the antibiotics prescribed for him were slow to have any effect, and as he was restless at night with a high temperature, I put up a camp bed in his room to reassure him and to dose him periodically with cough medicine. His crying usually brought on a paroxysm of coughing, so sometimes I took him into my bed to comfort him. I held him, rubbing his back gently, until his feverish little body relaxed into sleep.

During his illness, I also started to take him into the bath with me and, as Esme protested at what she considered partiality, she came in too. It was a tight fit for three of us, but it allowed me to have very close physical contact, which he didn't resist. Gradually he improved, coughed less and began to play with what seemed some enjoyment. One morning, leaving him asleep, I went downstairs to make a cup of tea. Coming back upstairs, I heard him talking to himself. In his bedroom, he was standing up in his cot. I pulled the curtains and turned to find him looking directly at me. He stretched his arms out and said, "Up, up!"

I lifted him out, saying, "Hello, sweetheart. How are you today?" and he put his arms around my neck.

"Mummy," he said, against my cheek. "Mummy." It was a moment of the purest joy. Once I had broken through his resistance, I found him a clingingly affectionate and lovable little boy. It was unsurprising that he had rejected me so comprehensively at the beginning. All the women in his life, whether good or bad, with whom he had had some form of relationship, had abandoned him. First his mother, then a temporary placement with a short-term foster mother, then a longer term placement with the foster mother that we met – all of them had passed out of his life in the blink of an eye. So why should he have had any confidence in me?

There was still some residual reticence in his interaction with others. He often stood on the edge of a circle of children, watching carefully, and was slow to join in, but his nature was friendly, even if it took a moment or so to overcome his uncertainty.

We began to settle down as a family, and in early summer took a boat holiday on the Thames with Mum and Dad. The children thought it magical, playing at houses on something that moved along the river. They loved the cabins and their bunk beds and even the basic showers. John explained the locks and how they worked, and the children were eager to help with the gates. They rushed into their grandparents' cabin each morning and had fun and cuddles. Dad usually escaped and made us all morning tea.

We fed ducks and their innumerable broods of ducklings, and the distinctly aggressive swans, with bread and, if they were lucky, stale cake. We moored wherever the fancy took us and shouted hello to the people we passed going the other way. The children loved that more than anything. I watched Paul begin to blossom a little. In the evening, before bedtime, Mum played board games and read them stories. Then when they were in bed, we four settled down to have dinner, chat and enjoy a drink or two before we too staggered to bed, sleepy with fresh air and wine.

"Can we come again next week?" was Esme's question when our holiday was over. Like all children, she always hated it when the things she was enjoying were coming to an end. In such circumstances she would often whisper to me, "Is it nearly finished?" Not because she wanted it to be, but in order to relish what was happening at the moment, and to know how much longer she had to enjoy it.

"Maybe next year; Daddy's got to go to work to earn enough money to afford it."

"But the ducks won't have anyone to feed them." She was ready to be tearful.

"They'll all come to Langstone and you will see them there next time you go there."

Dad disapproved of what he called deceiving the children. I pointed out that we had seen mallard on the Thames and there were mallard at Langstone. As the crow flies the distance was not enormous, so they could perfectly easily be the same birds, and who was to say they weren't?

Later in August, Mum and I took the children to the caravan in Walberswick where, among other things, we taught them the delights of crabbing. They were enchanted by the whole procedure. Those crabs must have become the worst-tempered crustaceans on the east coast. They spent most of their time being hauled out of the Blyth Estuary, clinging to crabbing lines, and then being scooped into nets inexpertly wielded by excited children, only to be dumped summarily into a large bucket of muddy water, where they wrestled for supremacy with all their fellow crabs. At the end of the day, they were tipped out onto the banks to scuttle back into the water, only for the whole thing to start again the next time. The trade-off was that they gorged to their hearts' content on rotten bacon and even more putrid fish heads, the bait of choice, supplied by the local fishermen on both sides of the estuary, so if they were the worst tempered, they were also the best fed!

Esme once put her hand incautiously into the bucket in order to fish out a particularly fine specimen she had hooked, to show her grandmother. Despite the absence of one of its claws she got her finger nipped for her trouble. Her howls were more of outrage than of pain.

There were other children on the caravan site to play with; John's cousin Sarah had twins, two little girls older than Esme and Paul, but clearly eager to play. Like many children, they loved bossing smaller ones about, but were just as happy to join the crabbing parties. We were rowed across the harbour to Blackshore by the ferryman, who always had his dog snoozing under his seat, which Esme thought amazing. "A dog on a boat, Mummy!" We walked into Southwold for ice-cream and other staples. We stayed a fortnight, as the weather was good, and we returned home brown and happy.

We had no idea of what lay ahead.

CHAPTER 31

The Storm

Paul had been with us for a year, and we were beginning to wonder when to apply to adopt him, when Social Services contacted us with devastating news. Alice phoned to say she needed to see us.

On arrival I thought she looked uneasy. She was very direct. "There's something you need to know. There have been some developments regarding Paul's mother. She has written to the department and applied to re-establish contact with him." At my gasp she continued hastily, "I'm on your side and I will oppose it, but my boss, I have to tell you, is inclined to be sympathetic to the request."

We listened to this astonishing disclosure in appalled silence. Overcome with horror I couldn't say a word, but John asked quietly, "With what aim?"

"It seems she has got married to a young naval rating. She says he's Paul's father, although his name is not on the birth certificate." She added quietly, "I must say, Paul looks quite like him." There was a long silence; she went on, "Initially, I think, she just wants to see him. But from what I gather, she hopes eventually to have him returned to her. She presents very well, you know: very much the reformed character. She and her new husband have naval quarters – nice little flat, all very proper!"

"But the judge said it was a terrible case of emotional abuse – the worst he'd heard of; that Paul had no future with her. He made a court order." I heard my voice, so shrill and disembodied I wasn't sure if I had actually spoken. The words seemed to be coming from somewhere and someone else.

"Yes, but she can appeal, and the order could be overturned; she hasn't signed anything yet. We have to hear what she has to say. I'm just painting a worst-case scenario. I don't think you need to be too anxious at the moment. I mean, she's got to prove her case and Paul lives with you, so that gives you, for the moment, the trump card. I am so sorry, but you had to know."

I looked at our little boy playing happily with his toy trains, completely oblivious to the drama unfolding around him. I couldn't take it in, and was gripped by sudden fear. "Does she know where he is? Can she find out?"

"No: you are quite safe in that respect."

John said slowly, "Let me get this straight. Social Services, the adoption department or whatever they are called, are contemplating taking this child – this child who has been in our care for nearly a year, who is fully integrated into our family, who is safe, secure and happy now, and who was severely traumatized and quite disturbed when he came to us – and returning him to a neglectful and abusive mother, a mother so deficient in her duties that he was removed from her and made the subject of a court order. That's what your boss is planning?"

"Nothing has been decided. This has got to go to the committee. All I am telling you is that Paul's mother has asked to re-establish contact with him. Her request has to be discussed. She has that right in law. Every decision taken must have Paul's best interests at heart. As I said, I shall oppose it. In the meantime I recommend you begin to marshal your defence. Write to the head of the Department of Social Services for Portsmouth and for Hampshire, and put your case."

"I'll do a damn sight more than that," said John angrily. "I'll write to my MP and every national newspaper in Britain. I'll blow this wide open. Do they want another Maria Colwell [the three-year-old returned from care to her mother's house only to be brutally abused and finally murdered by her stepfather] on their hands? Paul was placed with us with a view to adoption! What's changed? Any mother can turn up and say they are a changed person, and you return their abused child to them; is that what you do?"

When Alice left, I sat in dumb misery, her words swirling around in my mind. My brain felt sluggish; it was difficult to process or to make sense of what had been said. She had tried to reassure us, to comfort us, but I was icy with horror. Paul's best interests! What did that mean? Surely his best interests were to stay with us. Wild thoughts flashed through my mind. I would run away with him; go to Scotland or France; maybe the nuns would hide us. I had a momentary vision of Mother Henrietta and Mary-Mount. Would she take us in? Somehow I didn't think she would, and anyway we would be so easy to find.

John, with his usual analytical assessment, calmed me down. "We will win this, Tiny. We are more motivated. We are more articulate. We are more stable and we want it more. She may lose interest; she may not have the support she needs. I will talk to personnel at the office tomorrow and get advice, and in the evening we will draft some letters."

The next few days were agonizing. We resisted calling Alice. She had promised to let us know when the case would be discussed, and the outcome. We were confused. There was a difficulty in knowing who was batting for whom. Alice was in fact Paul's social worker, so if the meeting decided that Paul was better off with his mother, she had no option but to work toward that aim. Yet apparently she represented our interests too.

"It's madness," I fumed. I was beginning to move from despair to fury, and as I calmed I became coldly determined to win this battle – not for me, but for the little boy who in his grief had whispered the name of the little cat Daisy, the sweet memory of his lost world. I was determined to the very depth of my soul that this would not happen again. I dropped into my local church to speak to my parish priest. He was reassuring and sympathetic.

"I can't imagine they'll take Paul away from a happy and stable home where he is safe, loved and secure, and return him to some poor girl with a history of neglectful parenting."

"But Father, they do. That's the point. They took that little girl Maria Colwell away from happy caring foster parents and returned her to a feckless mother and a brutal stepfather. It could happen all over again."

"I'm sure it won't," he said firmly.

Where do they get all this certainty from, I wondered? *This priest is a nice man and wants to comfort and reassure me, and he's failing to do either.* I knew it wasn't his fault.

"Do you know Thomas More's prayer, composed on the eve of his execution? He talks about leaning into God's comfort. I think you might try that. Oh, and have a quick word with Our Lady. She really understands family issues! I mean, Jesus himself went AWOL aged twelve on the way back from Jerusalem. I think she too will comfort you. Isn't she 'our life, our sweetness and our hope'? If anyone is in a valley of tears, it's you."

The lovely words of the Salve Regina comforted me, but they also toughened my resolve. We were ready, John and I, to play dirty if necessary. The terrible, threatening whisperings – where I felt I was being pursued by malevolent creatures wearing the faces of our charming social worker and some unknown but beautiful young woman crying "mine, mine, mine" – that seemed to drum through my brain when I tried to sleep, began to fade. I felt a steely determination to win, no matter what I might have to do.

We planned our strategy ruthlessly. If this, then that; if this other, then that other. We decided we would default on meetings: go out for the day, express regret that we had forgotten, plead illness, suggest another date, be on holiday, and all the time write letters. Our aggressive response seemed to puzzle the Head of Hampshire Social Services Child Protection team, who asked with what seemed to us breathtaking naivety and, as we felt in our anguish, a total failure to understand our position, "Why are the Richardsons so angry?"

Alice kept us in touch with what was happening. The first worrying news was that the natural mother had been offered a date for a further meeting. We lived through that day in sweating anxiety. Alice phoned us in the evening. "She's turned it down, saying she couldn't make it. She's been given another date next week." I was limp with anti-climax.

"No, no," John said soothingly. "This is good. The longer we spin it out the better. I think she'll get tired. Some people just can't look to the long term; they want it instantly, otherwise they lose interest. I'm sure she probably does want him back. If she could have had him the day she first requested him, she'd have taken him, probably with great happiness, but to have to fight, to go to meetings, to explain, to justify – it's probably beyond her."

Listening to my husband, part of me felt sad for this poor young woman. At least she did want to try again, to make amends. We just couldn't tell. She'd got a husband, a flat and a degree of respectability; maybe the child added to that picture of domestic normality that she might have craved.

At the second meeting it was the alleged father, we were told, who turned up, on his own, explaining that his wife was too upset by the whole thing to attend. Alice said that he was a pleasant young man who wanted to make his new wife happy. As for himself, he didn't mind one way or the other about the baby. "That attitude doesn't strengthen their case," she explained. "He is not claiming fatherhood. He says his *wife* says it's his son! He doesn't know, but he's prepared to believe her. I'm sorry; this wait must be awful for you. They have been given another date in two weeks, and she has been told she must attend."

The frustrating and anxious wait of two weeks was very harrowing. Family and friends were supportive, and a local city councillor offered as much advice as he felt able, mainly to sit tight and wait. The days passed, the children played, we all ate, drank and slept, and on the surface our family life continued normally.

The day of the meeting arrived and Alice phoned with an account of the situation. A meeting had taken place. A repeated request for access had been made but with some aggression, which was viewed, Alice said, with disapprobation. The meeting had ended acrimoniously.

"Good!" said John. "What now?"

"We are looking at our own position."

"What position's that?"

"How best to move forward."

"You see," said my husband, "we are in this awful position where we don't know who is looking to our situation. I do realize," he went on hastily, "that Paul's needs are paramount, but surely, currently this child's needs are irrevocably bound up with his family home, which is here. So we do have, if you like, some vested interest."

Conversations went back and forth, questions and answers; it all seemed surreal and we were both becoming so tired. My nocturnal demons were back too, taunting me with ridiculous thoughts about the relative thickness of blood and water. This was all going on, floating above the soft, light brown hair of a little boy who called us "Mummy" and "Daddy" and who had a little sister and four affectionate grandparents.

We didn't know or care to hazard a guess as to how long this situation would continue. Did it mean that every six months or so, depending on the changing circumstances, Paul's natural mother could return for another attempt to regain him? In theory, yes; only adoption could put an end to it. Alice's assurance that there would ultimately be a decision was almost as worrying; what if it went in favour of re-establishing contact and against adoption? What if we were left just fostering?

Then after several weeks of living in limbo something quite unexpected happened. A certain sailor was sent to sea on a six-month deployment, and a young woman, with many problems of her own, found life on the naval housing estate without a handsome husband to support and sustain her very unappealing. Dying of boredom, she drifted back to her Portsmouth circle and melted out of Social Services' light beam. She became elusive and evasive and, having left no forwarding address, became non-contactable. Enquiries among her friends as to her whereabouts resulted in vague and uncertain suggestions, and they all drew a blank.

"There could be no better time," suggested Alice, "to apply to adopt. Her behaviour really seems to suggest lack of true intent. It might have been something she just felt she ought to do; a gesture. I am going to propose to the committee that we serve adoption papers."

John, ever cautious, pointed out that getting too excited could backfire, so we struggled for calm. All the paperwork was finalized by Social Services and despatched to her last known address. Unsurprisingly it was returned "unknown".

"If you can't find her," I asked Alice despairingly, "how can you serve adoption papers? Don't they need her signature?"

"We can, in view of her actions, apply to the court to make the decision anyway. We can, or rather the court can, dispense with her signature."

It all seemed so possible suddenly; why had it taken such an age? I thought of Esme's trouble-free passage through the courts. The slight run-in with the social workers over our rights to information seemed little more than a hiccup now. This long agony with Paul had kept us frantic with fear and rage, and yet was finally unnecessary. It all evaporated.

We went to the court as a family, with Mum and Dad and Esme. I had a momentary final panic that someone I had never seen, but who had haunted my sleep so that I had a perfect mind picture, would turn up, and as in my dreams scream, "He's mine: mine." No such apparition appeared.

Alice shepherded us into the antechamber where we were to meet the judge. He was as unlike Esme's affable, rotund and jolly fellow as he could possibly be: a lean, gaunt and unsmiling individual who looked as if he suffered from permanent dyspepsia. He took a long time rustling through the papers on his desk, dropping some, which were hastily picked up by the clerk who looked as sheepish as if he'd dropped them himself, and spent a few minutes in muttered conversation with Alice. He was taciturn to the point of incivility. He disappeared into the inner sanctum, beckoning to Alice and saying abruptly, "Would the prospective parents and the child please follow."

John caught up with him at the door. "We'd like to bring our daughter in with us. She was too young to know anything about her own adoption; she might remember this one, which could be helpful for her, and anyway we hope that she will, in a few moments, be Paul's sister."

"Just parents and child," was the surly response. He didn't even look at John. In the chambers we all sat down. Alice stood up to outline the situation: the mother's lack of co-operation and her disappearance making it impossible to serve her with the notice of intended adoption. She paused to reiterate a point, and John rose and said quietly, "I'm going to get my daughter." Ignoring everybody's startled glance he left the room. He returned a moment or two later with Esme, her little hand tucked into his. He told me afterwards, "I was damned if I was going to be overruled on that!" The judge raised pained eyebrows but said nothing, so by tacit consent our daughter stayed to see it through.

She got her little brother and Paul finally became our son when we heard the judge, with a warmer note to his voice, state our parental relationship. I was filled with such explosive happiness. It was only the hint of a drip on the end of that aquiline nose that prevented me from throwing my arms around him. I certainly hugged John and Alice, and then my little son and daughter, who looked bemused and not a little anxious. A tearful mother is always an unsettling situation.

"Don't cry, Tiny," advised John, his own eyes full. "It will upset our nibos" (the tender family name for the children).

Mum and Dad were waiting patiently outside and beamed with joy. "Do I say congratulations?" asked Mum, a little anxiously.

"Yes, of course," I replied. "Let's go home and open the champagne! We will drink to the Richardson family and Paul David, son of this house."

Epilogue

I lay in bed at the end of that stupendous day and listened to my husband's steady breathing and the gentle irregular creaking of the house around me. Eleven years since I had left Liverpool, nearly twenty since I had set off for France to enter the Noviciate, full of misplaced confidence and all the arrogant certainty of youth. Those years in my convent had been good to and for me. They had given me stability, security and a moral compass. They had trained me as a nurse and a midwife, capable of earning a good living. I had formed lifelong friendships.

In the years that followed, stability and security were once again thrown into question and the moral compass became ambivalent. For some time I was adrift, buffeted about by my desire for instant gratification and my failure to differentiate between transient emotion and durable loving affection. Despite my ebullient persona I had wrestled with more than one demon.

Friends had been kinder to me than I sometimes deserved. The thing I loved most about community life was just that: the company of the sisters. So friendship outside the convent was very precious. I could have fallen among thieves, but instead, happily, I fell among companions. When I met John he became the epicentre of my life, and his family a blanket, a palisade, a bastion of safety.

My irresponsible behaviour had deprived not just me, but John too, of natural children. Although he said, laughingly, that given our relevant personalities a child from our gene pool would have had to overcome very difficult character traits, I had many regrets about my failure to give him offspring of his own. My Catholic tendency to guilt I found hard to put down. I had to keep remembering the words of the priest who gave us lectures on moral philosophy: guilt, he had said, was pathological and had nothing to do with regret or contrition. Mental hospitals were full of people who were consumed with guilt, and some of the worst human beings had felt no guilt at all for their appalling actions.

Once we had two children my guilt seemed inappropriate and self-indulgent. I couldn't undo my folly or reclaim those years, but we had now in our care two beloved children; children we had yearned and fought for. Even Esme's straightforward adoption had had its moments of anguish and alarm, and for Paul it had been a monumental struggle of unimaginable distress and fear.

These wonderful children would teach me the value of love and the depth to which it could scour your heart. I realized that I would never again be free. Love would bind me to them all – John, Esme and Paul – and I was overwhelmingly happy to be so bound.

The first part of Eleanor's story can be found in...

Kicking the Habit

If you liked Call the Midwife, you'll love *Kicking the Habit!*

An upbeat, honest, funny but always affectionate portrait of convent life and hospital life in 1960s Britain

What makes a fun-loving teenager turn her back on a life of parties, boys and fun, to become a nun in a French convent? And what later leads her to abandon the religious life, to return to the big wide world and later marry?

At the age of 18, Eleanor Stewart goes to France to enter a convent. After four years of struggling with the religious life, she becomes a nun, and then trains as a midwife in a large inner-city hospital in Liverpool. While Beatlemania grips the nation, she attempts to coordinate the reclusive demands of the religious life with the drama, excitement and occasional tragedy of the hospital world. Written with honesty and affection, this is a wonderful and intimate portrait of convent and hospital life.

Published by Lion Books
ISBN 978-0-7459-5611-4